PROBLEM-BASED LEARNING

and

OTHER CURRICULUM MODELS

for the

MULTIPLE INTELLIGENCES
CLASSROOM

Robin Fogarty

SkyLight
Professional
Development

Arlington Heights, Illinois

**Problem-Based Learning and Other Curriculum Models
for the Multiple Intelligences Classroom**

Published by SkyLight Professional Development
2626 S. Clearbrook Dr., Arlington Heights, IL 60005
800-348-4474 or 847-290-6600
Fax 847-290-6609
info@skylightedu.com
http://www.skylightedu.com

Creative Director: Robin Fogarty
Managing Editor: T. B. Zaban
Editor: Monica Phillips
Graphic Designer: Bruce Leckie
Cover and Illustration Designer: David Stockman
Production Supervisor: Bob Crump
Production Assistant: Christina Georgi

ISBN 1-57517-067-1
LCCCN 96-77876

1921V
Item # 1464
Z Y X W V U T S R Q P O N M L K J I H G F E
06 05 04 03 02 01 00   15 14 13 12 11 10 9 8 7 6 5

To Dara Lee (Dee Dee) Howard,
the best problem solver I know.

Acknowledgments

My gratitude and thanks to the many people who helped make this publication real. In particular, my appreciation goes to Kay Burke for continuing the conversation about integrated learning, which led to this book, and to Valerie Moye for her enthusiasm and encouragement in promoting problem-based learning and thematic units.

As always, a special note to Brian, whose support and care are unending, and to my team of professionals at IRI/SkyLight, who have brought the ideas to fruition.

Contents

6 PERFORMANCE LEARNING 125

CLASSROOM EXAMPLES

	Elementary School	Middle School	High School
Problem-Based Learning	*Your Vote Counts* (voting responsibility) p. 11	*Designer Genes* (posthole: genetic engineering) p. 15	*It's Out There!* (outdoor education experience) p. 19
Case Studies	*"You're Not the Boss of Me!"* (authority, responsibility, independence, loyalty) p. 34	*A Lie Is a Lie Is a Lie* (truth, integrity, honesty) p. 36	*Who Says?* (censorship, bias, rights) p. 38
Thematic Learning	*It's a Seed of an Idea* (family tree, growth, roots) p. 61	*Rites of Passage: Rights or Responsibilities?* (growing up, rights, freedoms) p. 65	*Do You Mind My Habits of Mind?* (flexibility, craftsmanship, interdependence, efficacy, consciousness) p. 69
Project Learning	*Biography: Puppet and Presentation* (genre-related project) p. 87	*The Many Ways of Knowing Our Community* (template project) p. 90	*Cataboom* (structured project) p. 93
Service Learning	*Save a Park* (students work with park district to beautify local park) p. 108	*Violence: How Can We Kill It?* (students work with police to set up a neighborhood-watch program) p. 112	*Old Folks' Tales to Tell* (students "adopt" a grandparent from a local nursing home) p. 116
Performance Learning	*Tumbling* (P.E. demonstration on Parent Night) p. 137	*"How to" Speech* (class presentation) p. 139	*"The Decades in Review"* (musical production) p. 142

Foreword

We live in what is called an "age of possibility." Our political leaders urge us to "build bridges" to the twenty-first century and prepare ourselves for the challenges of a new millennium. Some educators suggest that we shift our paradigms of schooling from environments that demand conformity to rigid teaching and learning structures, to ones where students take command of their own education. In the latter paradigm, learning is more authentic and students are doing what Piaget suggests learning results from—acting upon reality.

Robin Fogarty's comprehensive and challenging new book, *Problem-Based Learning and Other Curriculum Models for the Multiple Intelligences Classroom,* outlines curriculum structures that embody the kinds of possibilities we need to make the educational, social, and psychological transition to the new century. They call upon us as educators to modify how we regard our subject matter and how we relate it to students and others in our schools.

Control of the curriculum is at the heart of each of the six curricular models discussed in this book. Traditionally, teachers have controlled decisions about what to study, how to study it, and what it all means. Fogarty challenges this historically dominant paradigm by suggesting that students can make important curricular and instructional decisions—they can be involved in posing and resolving problems in significant and meaningful ways.

With these six curriculum models, teachers and students assume new roles. Students become self-directed, responsible participants in the classroom while figuring out problems, responding to case studies, and engaging in service projects. Students no longer passively accept and return knowledge the teacher has passed on. Instead, they are active inquirers, researching ideas important to each subject area. They are engaged in authentic, complex situations that demand the highest levels of inquiry, critical analysis, and reflection. And, at times, they even act as teachers, while the teachers assume roles as coaches, facilitators, and learners.

As we approach the millennium, we need models of instruction that provide us—teachers, students, administrators, parents, and community members—with opportunities that challenge students to think creatively and productively about authentic problems and issues confronting our diverse society. Fogarty's book is an outstanding resource for fashioning this new vision of what teachers and students working together can achieve.

JOHN BARELL
MONTCLAIR STATE UNIVERSITY

Introduction

Two distinct arenas of research are impacting the educational scene: brain research and school reform. Existing research on the brain focuses on how the mind constructs meaning (Caine and Caine 1991), the many forms of cognition, and how we express knowledge (Gardner 1983). This research is complemented by the voices of school reform (Goodlad 1983; Sizer 1992; Boyer 1984), who advocate models of schooling that embrace more learner-centered structures. These structures include uninterrupted chunks of class time, teams of teachers working collaboratively, and groups of kids learning together over time. The implications of these ideas manifest themselves in educational innovations such as block scheduling, multiage classrooms, and year-round education. These innovations show that we are making a gradual shift in how instruction, assessment, and curriculum, in particular, are being approached.

Curricular reform plays a key role in the migration toward holistic, integrated, and brain-compatible models of learning. If instruction and assessment are the cornerstone of what really happens with learners in the classroom, then curriculum is the foundation of the school programs. It is the curriculum that determines what and how teachers spend their instructional time in the classroom. It is the curricular focus that dictates what is tested, assessed, and evaluated, both formatively and summatively.

What Comes First? Assessment or Instruction?

The saying "assessment drives instruction" refers to a well-known and widely accepted practice of teachers "teaching to the test" (or tests), and rightly so. If teachers know what their students are going to be held accountable for, they have an obligation to prepare their students in those areas. For example, if teachers know that students are going to be tested on the state constitution, teachers target the constitution as a priority topic. In addition, if the test is designed to assess a student's recall of facts, data, and information, then teachers spend their time helping students become proficient at recalling facts, data, and information.

However, what is often not considered is that the tests are based on *someone's* view of the valued curriculum. If the state constitution is on the test, then *someone* has determined that the state constitution is worth knowing about. In turn, if *someone* determines that the actual assessments should focus on recall rather than reasoning, then the instructional time also focuses on recall, because that is what is most likely to guarantee success for the students being tested. Consider now a reverse axiom regarding assessment as stated by Eisner (1985), "If it's not worth teaching, it's not worth testing. First, we must decide what's worth teaching." That's where curriculum comes in.

Because the curriculum is the foundation of instruction and assessment, valued learner qualities and content must be determined before any substantive discussions about instruction and assessment begin. A curriculum rich in conceptual content, life skills, and processes, and which has integrity, dictates the same kind of instruction and assessment.

Consider the state constitution discussed earlier. If the tests focus on reasoning rather than recall, students must thoughtfully problem-solve authentic situations involving the state constitution. Therefore, teachers must earnestly prepare students in rigorous and multidimensional applications of the constitutional principles. This shift in the focus of testing occurs only if and when the following occurs: *someone* values reasoning as well as recall in the curriculum; the curriculum requires students to approach real problematic situations; expectations are set for students to learn to work through the problems, consider the alternatives, and advocate solutions; and the assessments are designed in such a way that students are asked to perform these kinds of authentic tasks.

When these criteria are met, instruction and assessment become synchronized with the goals of a strong curriculum.

Curricular Frameworks

This book presents a survey of six curricular frameworks for problem-based learning developed in conjunction with Gardner's theory of multiple intelligences: problem-based learning, case studies, thematic learning, project learning, service learning, and performance learning. Figure 1 provides a quick reference to the stages involved in each curricular model.

Problem-Based Learning

Problem-based learning (PBL) is a curricular model that uses an authentic problem as the impetus for learning. It begins with an ill-structured, open-ended problem, such as the controversy at one middle school about what its students really need to learn. This problem

Curricular Models: Phases of Development

Problem-Based Learning	Case Studies	Thematic Learning	Project Learning	Service Learning	Performance Learning
Meeting the problem	Key Concepts	Brainstorming a bank of themes	First-story intellect: Gathering activities	Selecting the need for service	The Prompt
Defining the problem	Content/Disciplines	Posing questions	• Read	Finding a community partner	The Vision
Gathering the facts	Compelling narrative	Turning a theme into a problem-solving investigation	• Research	Aligning service with educational goals	The Standards
• Know			• Interview		
• Need to know	Facts	• Gathering facts	• View		The Coaching
• Need to do			• Listen	Managing the project	Context
	Small group discussions	• Analyzing the problem	• Visit	• Planning	• Explanation
Hypothesizing			• Search Internet	• Monitoring	• Demonstration
	Debriefing		Second-story intellect: Processing activities	• Evaluating	• Feedback
Researching		• Generating alternatives	• Sketch		• Performance
	Follow-up		• Draw	Fostering reflective learning	• Reflection
Rephrasing the problem		• Advocating a solution or position	• Calculate		
			• Generate		The Presentation
Generating alternatives			• Develop a prototype		
					The Reflection
Advocating solutions			Third-story intellect: Applying activities		
• Probable			• Try		
• Possible			• Test		
• Preferable			• Evaluate		
			• Revise		
			• Repeat the cycle		
			• Showcase		

Figure I

leads students to an investigation from which subject matter content and instruction springs. PBL may be the entire focus of a course, or it may occur within the context of a unit of study, which is called "post-holing." As a curricular framework, PBL provides a genuine context for relevant learning.

Case Studies

Case studies, rooted in philosophy and law, use real cases to ferret out essential learnings. The case study is introduced through a vignette or scenario. Students then discern the facts and analyze and crystallize the issues through Socratic dialogue. Often moral and ethical issues are framed around situational dilemmas in which ambiguity and paradox play major roles. Just as in life, the issues are not always black and white. They tap the core of our value system as we search for viable answers. For instance, as students grapple with the ideas of authority vs. individual rights in regard to gun regulation, they confront their own values. Case studies provide a holistic curricular frame that immerses students in relevant learning experiences.

Thematic Learning

Thematic learning involves using a "big idea" theme as a curriculum organizer. For example, "patterns" is a theme that can be used creatively. Targeted content, skills, and attitudes are easily organized under the umbrella of "patterns." Students can find patterns in an earth science unit or create tessellations to study design in math and art. The idea of patterns can be used to look at American history, government, and economics. It is also a way to study poetry, literature, and music. It's rich. It's fertile. It's inviting. That's the appeal of thematic learning as a framework for curriculum.

Project Learning

Project learning uses a complex project as the catalyst for instruction. The curricular frame of project learning provides the reason for learning abstract ideas and principles. They become relevant, concrete tools. For example, high school students integrate the Pythagorean theorem from their math class to their vocational education project—erecting the frame of a house. Students gain a deep understanding of the theorem as they use their knowledge of right triangles to build the frame of a real house. While not all projects are this extensive, project learning is a curricular model that promotes student interest and involvement.

Service Learning

Service learning is a curricular framework that involves students in a community project or program. It puts kids in "service" to a community so they can learn in an authentic context. For example, students may become part of a civic program to clean up a local river or wipe out graffiti in their neighborhoods. Students work with each other and with local agencies to rally their efforts for a common cause. Just as with project learning, service learning acts as a magnet for content and skills. Students are drawn to the learning because the context has real meaning. Service learning gives purpose to experiences both inside and outside of the classroom.

Performance Learning

Performance learning is learning by doing. It's about immersing students in the act of performing an actual learning task. One well-known example of performance learning is driver's education. Students are placed in a simulation in which they must perform a set of tasks in order to demonstrate that they can drive a car. Eventually, after ample rehearsal, they practice doing the driving tasks in an actual car. Performance learning requires depth of knowledge and deep understanding that is evidenced through the performance itself. As a curricular frame, performance learning is useful in the lab setting, the visual and performing arts, and classroom hands-on learning situations that require students to demonstrate what they know.

Multiple Intelligences

The curricular models discussed in this book shape learning and assessment in K–college classrooms. Each model is designed with multidimensional strategies and versatile tools that help operationalize Gardner's theory of multiple intelligences. In addition to Gardner's seven intelligences, the models also include the newly discussed intelligence—the naturalist, or the intelligence of the physical world.

Just as Gardner (1983) suggests, the intelligences seldom work in isolation. In holistic learning experiences, they are interrelated to each other. This is true for the models discussed in this book. For example, students may use their *logical/mathematical* intelligence to think through a situation; their *visual/spatial* intelligence to visualize it; their *interpersonal* intelligence to empathize with people; their *intrapersonal* intelligence to reflect on a similar personal situation; and their *bodily/kinesthetic* intelligence to immerse themselves in a situation through an experiential learning process. The *musical/rhythmic* and *verbal/linguistic* intelligences may come into play as students use music to depict the mood or tone of a problem and discuss, write, listen, and read about related issues. In addition, students use their *naturalist* intelligence to classify and organize objects in their natural surroundings.

Following is a brief description of each intelligence. In addition, figures 2–4 provide a quick reference for transferring the multiple intelligences theory to the classroom. For a more in-depth look at Gardner's theory, refer to the bibliography for resources that are both theoretical and practical.

Visual/Spatial

This is the intelligence of the artist, designer, architect, the child who loves jigsaw puzzles, and the amateur astronomer. The visual/spatial intelligence translates ideas into images, pictures, illustrations, drawings, maps, and graphic representations. The visual/spatial intelligence manifests itself in the "mind's eye" through vivid imagination, dreaming, and conceptualizing. People with this intelligence envision things like sand paintings, sculptures, and skyscrapers.

Verbal/Linguistic

This intelligence involves reading, writing, listening, and speaking. Both oral and written language as evidenced in skillful communication and artful articulation are aspects of this intelligence. People graced with a high profile in the verbal/linguistic intelligence include trial lawyers, sales people, poets, statesmen, preachers, and teachers. The verbal/linguistic intelligence encompasses children tuned in to the world of literacy—the literature and stories of yesterday and the news and talk of the present day.

Logical/Mathematical

Those endowed with a high logical/mathematical intelligence are genetic scientists, physicists, engineers, mathematicians, organizational managers, chess enthusiasts, philosophers, and military strategists who excel in inductive and deductive reasoning. This intelligence speaks to the "reasoned voice" in each of us as we make sense of our surroundings. Children manifest this intelligence in their quest for logic and cause-and-effect reasoning.

Musical/Rhythmic

People with a strong musical/rhythmic intelligence sing, hum, whistle, or clap to songs. They are immersed in music in personally relevant ways—appreciating, composing, performing. The musical/rhythmic intelligence engages the whole of the person in the musical piece. Composers, blues singers, jazz musicians, classical pianists, guitar-strumming teens, choir members, band leaders, and youngsters singing childhood songs are all using their musical/rhythmic intelligence.

Bodily/Kinesthetic

Skilled athletes and talented keyboard operators both exhibit a strong bodily/kinesthetic intelligence. This intelligence is also found in carpenters, masons, and ornamental iron workers. It calls for hands-on learning, biology labs, computer keyboarding, dramatic role-plays, simulations, and immersion in automotive shop tasks. The bodily/kinesthetic intelligence retains the motor memory used to dial phone numbers, drive a car, ride a bike, or ski down a black diamond ridge.

Interpersonal/Social

Charismatic leaders, school psychologists, social workers, coaches, sales managers, and office receptionists all exhibit the interpersonal/social intelligence. This intelligence permits us to feel sympathy, compassion, and empathy. It allows us to compromise, collaborate, and care for people. The interpersonal intelligence helps one to create social bonds with friends, families, and whole communities. It summons the global village concept of the interrelatedness of the human race.

Intrapersonal/Introspective

The art of "knowing thyself" is at the heart of this intelligence. Self-awareness, self-understanding, self-reflection, self-monitoring, and self-assessing represent the intrapersonal/introspective intelligence. Poets, philosophers, counselors, ministers, artists, and authors are often strong in this intelligence.

Naturalist/Physical World

People who are strong in the naturalist/physical world intelligence have an understanding of the ecosystem. They know the intricacies and subtleties of the connectedness in nature. Naturalists include hikers, bird watchers, conservationists, and environmentalists. The naturalist/physical world intelligence helps one to classify sea shells and categorize deciduous and coniferous trees. It is the intelligence ruled by Mother Nature.

Conclusion

By using the holistic models discussed in this book, teachers can structure their curricula in ways that give them more time to teach their students. These curricular frameworks, along with the multiple intelligences theory, will encourage teachers, leaders, researchers, and educators to consider not only *what* they teach, but also *how* they teach it.

Gardner's Eight Intelligences

Visual/Spatial
Images, graphics, drawings, sketches, maps, charts, doodles, pictures, spatial orientation, puzzles, designs, looks, appeal, mind's eye, imagination, visualization, dreams, nightmares, films, and videos.

Logical/Mathematical
Reasoning, deductive and inductive logic, facts, data, information, spreadsheets, databases, sequencing, ranking, organizing, analyzing, proofs, conclusions, judging, evaluations, and assessments.

Verbal/Linguistic
Words, wordsmiths, speaking, writing, listening, reading, papers, essays, poems, plays, narratives, lyrics, spelling, grammar, foreign languages, memos, bulletins, newsletters, newspapers, E-mail, FAXes, speeches, talks, dialogues, and debates.

Musical/Rhythmic
Music, rhythm, beat, melody, tunes, allegro, pacing, timbre, tenor, soprano, opera, baritone, symphony, choir, chorus, madrigals, rap, rock, rhythm, and blues, jazz, classical, folk, ads and jingles.

Bodily/Kinesthetic
Art, activity, action, experiental, hands-on, experiments, try, do, perform, play, drama, sports, throw, toss, catch, jump, twist, twirl, assemble, disassemble, form, re-form, manipulate, touch, feel, immerse, and participate.

Interpersonal/Social
Interact, communicate, converse, share, understand, empathize, sympathize, reach out, care, talk whisper, laugh, cry, shudder, socialize, meet, greet, lead, follow, gangs, clubs, charisma, crowds, gatherings, and twosomes.

Intrapersonal/Introspective
Self, solitude, meditate, think, create, brood, reflect, envision, journal, self-assess, set goals, plot, plan, dream, write, fiction, nonfiction, poetry, affirmations, lyrics, songs, screenplays, commentaries, introspection, and inspection.

Naturalist
Nature, natural, environment, listen, watch, observe, classify, categorize, discern patterns, appreciate, hike, climb, fish, hunt, snorkle, dive, photograph, trees, leaves, animals, living things, flora, fauna, ecosystem, sky, grass, mountains, lakes, and rivers.

Figure 2

xx

IRI/SkyLight Training and Publishing

Ways to Experience Learning

Verbal	Visual	Logical	Musical	Interpersonal	Intrapersonal	Bodily	Naturalist
Reporting	Story-boarding	Reasoning	Singing	Discussing	Journaling	Dancing	Relating
Writing essays	Painting	Collecting	Listening	Responding	Intuiting	Sculpting	Discovering
Creating	Cartooning	Recording	Playing	Dialoguing	Reflecting	Performing	Uncovering
Reciting	Observing	Analyzing	Composing	Reporting	Logging	Preparing	Observing
Listing	Drawing	Graphing	Audio-taping	Surveying	Meditating	Constructing	Digging
Telling/retelling	Illustrating	Comparing/contrasting	Improvising	Questioning	Studying	Acting	Planting
Listening	Diagraming	Classifying	Attending concerts	Paraphrasing	Rehearsing	Role-playing	Comparing
Labeling	Depicting	Ranking	Selecting music	Clarifying	Self-assessing	Dramatizing	Displaying
Joking	Showing	Evaluating	Critiquing music	Affirming	Expressing	Pantomiming	Sorting

Figure 3

IRI/SkyLight Training and Publishing

Types of Activities

Verbal	Visual	Logical	Musical	Interpersonal	Intrapersonal	Bodily	Naturalist
Symbols	Mosaics	Mazes	Performance	Group projects	Journals	Role-playing	Field trips (farm/zoo)
Printouts	Paintings	Puzzles	Songs	Group tasks	Meditations	Dramatizing	Field studies
Debates	Drawings	Outlines	Musicals	Observation charts	Self-assessments	Skits	Bird watching
Poetry	Sketches	Matrices	Instruments	Social interactions	Intuiting	Body language	Observing nests
Jokes	Illustrations	Sequences	Rhythms	Dialogs	Logs	Facial expressions	Planting
Speeches	Cartoons	Patterns	Compositions	Conversations	Records	Experiments	Photographing
Reading	Sculptures	Logic	Harmonies	Debates	Reflections	Dancing	Nature walks
Storytelling	Models	Analogies	Chords	Arguments	Quotations	Gestures	Forecasting weather
Listening	Constructions	Timelines	Trios/Duos	Consensus	"I Statements"	Pantomiming	Star gazing
Audiotapes	Maps	Equations	Quartets	Communication	Creative expression	Field trips	Fishing
Essays	Storyboards	Formulas	Beat	Collages	Goals	Lab work	Exploring caves
Reports	Videotapes	Theorems	Melodies	Murals	Affirmations	Interviews	Categorizing rocks
Crosswords	Photographs	Calculations	Raps	Mosaics	Insight	Sports	Ecology studies
Fiction	Symbols	Computations	Jingles	Round robins	Poetry	Games	Catching butterflies
Nonfiction	Visual aids	Syllogisms	Choral readings	Sports	Interpretations		Shell collecting
Newspapers	Posters	Codes	Scores	Games			Identifying plants
Magazines	Murals	Games	Acappella choirs	Challenges			
Internet	Doodles	Probabilities					
Research	Statues	Fractions					
Books	Collages						
Biographies	Mobiles						
Bibliographies							

Figure 4

IRI/SkyLight Training and Publishing

PROBLEM-BASED LEARNING

A problem well stated is a problem half solved.
—Charles F. Kettering

Problem-Based Learning

What Is Problem-Based Learning?

Problem-based learning is a curriculum model designed around real-life problems that are ill-structured, open-ended, or ambiguous. An ill-structured problem is fuzzy, unclear, or not yet identified. It is often a situation that is confusing and complex, with a number of interrelated concerns. The problem may only be sensed at first. It is not fully delineated. For example, students or teachers may sense that there is a problem on the playground at lunchtime. However, they do not know exactly what the problem is.

Problem-based learning engages students in intriguing, real, and relevant intellectual inquiry and allows them to learn from these life situations (Barell 1995). Students become stakeholders, broaching problems as their own. In fact, one of the most distinctive elements of true problem-based learning is the students' ownership of the problem and the natural, student-directed way the problem unfolds.

What Does Problem-Based Learning Look and Sound Like?

Problem-based learning is, more often than not, presented to students through a nonfictional piece. This may take the form of a journal article, a brief factual entry, an expository piece in excerpted form, or simply a short scenario representing a situation. Once presented, students control the route the investigation takes.

Problem-based learning can be applied across the entire curriculum. The problem-based scenario dictates a comprehensive student investigation that is fluid, dynamic, flexible, and ever changing. An example of a dynamic problem that becomes a vehicle for learning is a scenario in which a family decides whether or not to place their grandfather in a nursing home.

Given a brief description of the situation, students undertake the investigation as though they are the family. In the process of investigating the problem, students learn about health, social studies, consumer math, government, law, communications, and the Internet.

Problem-based learning, as described in this chapter, can be either the total curriculum focus or just a part of the curriculum. Post-holing, however, is a form of problem-based learning that uses a problem as a temporary basis for in-depth learning. This type of problem-based learning stems from traditional curricular content. It is not the focus of the entire curriculum. For example, students may take a detour in a history unit to consider the government and the right to vote. They may discuss a present-day scenario, such as getting the African-American community to vote.

Although post-holing dictates a problem-based learning approach, its scope is contained to a brief period of time and is directly related to the current curricular unit. For example, while studying government systems, students may investigate the tobacco lobbyists' role in the election process. The post-holing method of problem-based learning is employed as a means of deepening students' understanding of key concepts in a predetermined curricular content. The problem is not the curriculum, but rather a dimension of the core of the curriculum.

**Problem-Based
Learning**

How Does Problem-Based Learning Work?

As stated earlier, problem-based learning starts with an ill-structured problem—a mess. From this initial mess, students use their many intelligences (Gardner 1983) through discussion and research to determine the real issue at hand. They then work to define the problem, gather known facts, generate questions, hypothesize, anticipate needed information, rephrase the problem, and, eventually, generate alternatives, advocate solutions, and justify recommendations. The process for approaching each problem depends on its structure, subject, and context. In authentic problem-based learning scenarios, the problem and the students determine the path the investigation follows. Following are some elements to consider when investigating a problem.

✳ Meeting the Problem

Students "meet the problem" through reading, role-playing, creating videos, writing raps, or any other number of creative methods using the multiple intelligences.

Just as in real-life, students may not know exactly what the problem is. In essence, the problem is ill-structured (Stepien et al. 1993). Open-ended problems are essential to problem-based learning. They are what distinguish this curriculum model from others.

The problem, or mess, is often presented through an ill-structured, open-ended, real-life scenario that describes a situation. The scenario may be

**Problem-Based
Learning**

quite short, giving few facts and only a brief statement of the circumstances. The introduction of the scenario includes the point of view to be assumed by the students. The scenario explicitly calls for a decision to the problem. Thus, the initial presentation of the problem presents all the vital information needed for the investigation. Students are armed with the key facts they need to begin.

However, the work begins in problem-based learning only after the students become stakeholders. When students become stakeholders, they experience the authenticity of the problem. They view the experience with the particular bias that is present in a real-life setting. By assuming a particular viewpoint, students must use their inter- and intrapersonal intelligences to seek to understand other viewpoints. Defining roles is critical to the problem-solving process. Roles provide a focus for the ensuing investigation and create an integrity of purpose that would otherwise be less than real. No real-world problem is seen objectively; every point of view comes with its own built-in bias. Thus, more authentic learning is ensured as the logic and/or faulty logic of the students' thinking unfolds.

For example, an ill-structured problem may involve a family faced with deciding whether or not an elderly family member should receive medical treatment, and if so, to what extent. In this scenario, students are instructed to take the role of the doctor, recommending alternatives to the family. Students can advise the "family" after using their multiple intelligences to reach a decision. Students can use their bodily/kinesthetic intelligence through experiential, hands-on learning; their interpersonal intelligence to interview others; their intrapersonal intelligence to reflect on the problem; and their logical/mathematical intelligence to reason logically.

✳ Defining the Problem

Once students get an understanding of the problem and become stakeholders, they attempt to state it in their own words. At this stage, the problem is only defined within the known parameters. The students understand that *several* definitions will have to be proposed as information becomes available. Therefore, the students' initial attempt at definition only allows them to understand based on what they know. However, once students are able to succinctly state the problem, they are able to steer the investigation in a direction that will lead them to additional information.

✳ Gathering the Facts

Students tap into their previous experiences and prior knowledge when gathering facts. They also use multiple intelligences to seek out information related to the problem. In teams, they use their talents to define the real issues and direct the investigation and decision.

In this phase, students must delineate what they know and what they need to know. Organizing this information using a "know, need to know, need to do" (KND) chart (Stepien et al. 1993) is helpful for students to analyze the problem and the facts related to it (see fig. 1.1).

Once the students list the facts they have accumulated, they need still more information. They begin to generate questions in an effort to determine what they still need to know. Particular facts, related information, and contextual understandings pop up continually during the questioning process. Sometimes, fact gathering is facilitated by the teacher/leader, who is skilled in questioning techniques. Other times, questions are generated by students or student teams. Of course, this depends on the age, experience, and sophistication of the problem solvers involved.

Problem-Based Learning

✳ Hypothesizing

As the fact-finding process advances, students focus on what they need to do. Using their logical/mathematical intelligence and reasoning abilities, students begin to theorize or hypothesize about the problem. Students also use their interpersonal intelligence to express what they think, what their hunches are, and what they sense the next logical steps or possible outcomes will be (Stepien and Gallagher 1993). As students tap into the myriad connections their minds are making, they probe for questions that will help them determine whether or not their hypotheses are true and whether they need to be refined in order to be considered valid.

✳ Researching

After gathering facts and listing pertinent questions, students can begin to research data and gather more information. The form this research takes depends on the nature of the problem. Reading textbooks, conducting personal interviews, surfing the Internet, browsing the library, visiting sites, and searching for related topics are all part of the research process that is the heart and soul of authentic problem-based learning. Research is an ongoing part of an investigation and is woven throughout problem-based learning. Mini-lessons in research techniques can be incorporated as needed.

The multiple intelligences are obvious tools of research. Students receive and express information in their own way. They combine their various intelligences in unique ways to make meaning of situations. Teachers structure learning to enable students to use their many ways of knowing and understanding their world. The problem-based model is an experiential one in which students deal with real-life situations through their diverse profiles of intelligence.

✳ Rephrasing the Problem

During the research stage, the initial problem statement is revised to reflect the emerging picture. For example, students may initially explore the problem of injuries on the playground, but end up discussing how to *design* a

KND Chart

What We **K**now	What We **N**eed to Know	What We Need to **D**o

Figure 1.1

6

IRI/SkyLight Training and Publishing

playground. This kind of shift often occurs. In this case, the students' research suggested that many of the injuries incurred on the playground were from fights between students. The students were fighting because there was not enough playground equipment for everyone.

The initial statement is devised from the "mess" presented early in the problem scenario. As the investigation progresses, more information is available; terminology is defined; and the inherent intricacies, complexities, and innuendoes of the circumstances emerge. Using the verbal/linguistic intelligence, students refine their statement of the problem in as precise language as possible. Doing this helps them refocus the investigation. Rephrasing the problem signals progress in learning because students zoom in on key ideas. With additional information, analysis of the data, and constant monitoring of the original problem base, the result is deep understanding of the object of intense scrutiny. Students dive into the problems and assume responsibility for knowing about every aspect of them. Thus, the teacher/leader encourages students to look at the problem statement from time to time. However, the teacher does not fully direct the problem-based process at any time. It is the students' responsibility to be productive throughout the entire experience. However, mini-lessons are used whenever the teacher determines a need for direct instruction in an area.

✳ Generating Alternatives

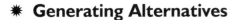

Students often collaborate as they discuss data and information relevant to the problem. Every student is a member of the problem-solving team and offers a unique perspective. Team members begin to grapple with the intricacies of the problem as legal, moral, ethical, and economic information is revealed. At this stage of the problem-solving process, generating alternatives in a think-tank model works better than individuals working alone. For example, de Bono (1992) tells of a problem scenario in which a newly erected skyscraper had inadequate elevators. After debating in a think-tank mode, the team's suggestions varied from redesigning the building to installing a helicopter pad on top. The final solution was quite surprising. The engineers and architects decided to install mirrored walls by the elevators on each floor. The team hypothesized that the people would be so busy looking at themselves in the mirrors, they wouldn't complain about the long wait. Their theory proved to be right! Through team thinking, the problem was solved in a cost-effective way.

Just as "real-life" problems are usually framed by time constraints, problem-based learning must also have timelines. Students must adhere to the parameters set at the outset of the problem-based scenario, which include the facts of the problem and the established timelines. Keeping the investigation aligned with the original parameters is part of the rigor of the process. If students need more time, they must do what it takes to change the timeline. For example, if the investigation takes an unexpected turn, delays may be prudent. More specifically, if students are working on a prob-

**Problem-Based
Learning**

lem scenario regarding Native American land rights, they may need time to investigate new information, such as a late-breaking court ruling on antiquities laws. However, if public forums are scheduled, timelines may be less flexible. This brings the authenticity of the experience to the learner.

Generating alternatives brings the investigative team, or stakeholders, together. They put several ideas on the table, and, just as in real-life situations, consider all of them to make the best possible decision. Students can explore alternatives by placing them into three distinct categories: *probable* solutions, *possible* alternatives, *preferable* resolutions. This process encourages stakeholders to examine every idea for its inherent worth. It can also delay impulsive decisions.

✳ Advocating Solutions

As students examine the alternatives and attempt to label them as *probable, possible,* or *preferable,* they may begin to realize which one has the most appeal and/or makes the most sense. The students, however, cannot assume that everyone will agree on the best decision. They must have candid discussions to comprehensively evaluate the options. Through a multiple intelligences approach, students must explore all avenues for the best solution. They may need to write, sketch, plot, discuss, and debate their ideas. Although certain alternative solutions may seem the most reasonable, the voice of reason isn't the only voice in the milieu of complex issues. There are also the voices of ethics, morality, spirituality, and emotion.

When it is time for the students to make a decision, they weigh each alternative and present the best solution. Team members in favor of the solution justify it to the other members. Those who don't agree with the solution may want to look at the other options again. The key attribute of problem-based learning is its dynamic nature. Things are always in flux, always fluid, just as they are in life. Circumstances change without warning, problems are redefined, solutions shift, new alternatives appear, and every aspect is open to reexamination at any moment in the process. Decisions are made and actions are taken based on the best thinking at that time. And, just as in life, one decision often leads to another set of circumstances that may require attention.

Who Are the Key Players and What Are Their Roles?

Students

The students are stakeholders, which allows them to become immersed in the problem as their own. This role is a critical element of problem-based learning that sets it apart from other curricular models involving problem solving. By taking on the roles of stakeholders, students examine the issues from a distinct and, by nature, biased perspective. Imagine the different views on teenage drinking as expressed by a parent, teenager, police officer, guidance counselor, or members of Mothers Against Drunk Driving (MADD), Students Against Drunk Driving (SADD), or the clergy.

Students also become the architects of their learning with the problem-based model. Unlike other curricular models, which are structured primarily by the teacher, problem-based learning is designed by the students. The unit of study, while encompassing certain generic phases, is determined by the nature of the problem. Of course, this does not give anyone license for total academic freedom. Because students have more responsibility and control over their own learning than in traditional models of curriculum, they need explicit coaching and guidance.

**Problem-Based
Learning**

Teachers

After the introduction of the problem, the teacher becomes the "guide on the side" rather than the "sage on the stage." The teacher facilitates the process as it develops by coaching, counseling, and directing as needed. However, the students are responsible for being productive at each stage. The teacher is there to help, but not to interfere in any way. Therefore, the teacher must genuinely believe in the process and in the students.

To get started, some teachers may want to use the post-holing model, which is a shorter version of the problem-based model and stresses deeper understanding within a unit of study. It is also less invasive of the curriculum and offers a compromise for teachers introducing problem-based learning. It is also a good model for those who prefer a traditional curriculum.

Why Does Problem-Based Learning Work?

In an effort to trace the research on problem-based learning and the evidence of its effectiveness as a curriculum model, Barrows' medical model (Barrows 1985) is the centerpiece of problem-based learning. Barrows devised the problem-based approach in an effort to design a clinical model for apprenticeships in the medical field. He used ill-structured problems that required the students to not only know a multitude of facts, but also to apply those facts to their diagnostic work. In effect, Barrows used the problem-based learning model as the catalyst for developing medical knowledge, problem-solving skills, and ongoing motivation for professional inquiry.

The problem-based learning approach for the classroom has been researched and used at the Center for Problem-Based Learning at the Illinois Math and Science Academy (Stepien and Gallagher 1993). Ill-structured problems are the basis for the two models taught in two courses at the academy, which are cited in their literature. Science, Society, and the Future is the name of one of the courses in which students use problem-based learning to tackle the social and ethical questions surrounding controversial scientific issues. The other course is in American studies. In this course, teachers

Problem-Based Learning

use the post-holing method of problem-based learning to deepen students' understanding of particular issues related to history.

John Barell (n.d.) has written about a contemporary view of problem-based learning in which problems emerge within the context of subject-matter content and students pursue the problem within the context of their learning. While similar to post-holing, Barell indicates that problem-based learning is an ongoing process that deepens learning throughout a unit of study. Thus, it is a middle-of-the-road approach to the problem-based model and the post-holing method.

While the literature on problem-based learning, per se, is scarce at best, its historical underpinnings date back to John Dewey's ([1938] 1963) work in experiential education at the University of Chicago Lab School in 1938. The writings of G. Polya (1988), while not specifically aligned with problem-based learning, emphasize metacognitive reflection on learned heuristics as a problem-solving tool. In Polya's model, students might review their steps to solving the problem, with an emphasis on extracting generalizable labels such as "visualizing" or "part-to-whole thinking." In addition, the current focus on authentic learning (Newmann and Wehlage 1993) further verifies the appeal of problem-based learning as an experiential model.

Writings on "higher-order thinking" also allude to problem-based learning. Grounded in the 1980s, when thinking-skills programs prevailed, this model of problem solving teaches students to think inductively and deductively (Feuerstein, Rand, Hoffman, and Miller 1980; de Bono 1976; Lipman, Sharp, and Oscanyan 1980; Costa 1985; Nickerson, Perkins, and Smith 1985; Marzano et al. 1988; Fogarty and Bellanca 1991; Paul 1987; Resnick 1987; Jones and Beyer 1987). It teaches students to think in the concrete and the abstract, moving through the stages of problem solving from novice to expert. Teachers use this model to develop rigorous thinking experiences for their students. While existing literature on higher-order thinking does not specifically refer to these experiences as problem-based learning, they certainly provide the cognitive basis for contemporary work in the area.

Writings on gifted education also represent early efforts in the area of problem-based learning. The roots of problem-based learning can be found in Parnes, Noller, and Biondi's work (1977) with the Creative Problem Solving Model, Torrence's work (1963) with the Future Problem Solving Bowl, and programs such as Olympics of the Mind and Renzulli's work (1979) with gifted education.

In more current literature, brain research findings published by Caine and Caine (1991) provide fertile ground for holistic models of curriculum that are brain compatible. In addition, the research supporting the constructivist theory of learning (Brooks and Brooks 1993), which argues that the learner constructs meaning in the mind by connecting prior knowledge to new learning, points toward problem-based learning as a viable curricular frame. Students immersed in problem-based learning are constantly trying to make meaning of the entire situation. It is a natural, brain-compatible model.

When Can Problem-Based Learning Be Used Effectively?

ELEMENTARY EXAMPLE
Your Vote Counts

✳ Meet the Problem

Electing government officials is a key element in a democratic society. Voting is both a right and a responsibility, and it is the people voting at the polls who determine the outcome of an election. Historically, certain groups, such as African Americans and women, have been denied the *right* to vote. However, today the issue seems to be more focused on the citizens' *responsibility* to vote. The following problem-based scenario focuses on political elections and the rights and responsibilities of citizens in the political process:

> You are the leader of a community group advocating voters' responsibility to get out and vote. Your grandmother, who lives in a nursing home, is eligible to vote in your district. However, she is unable to see well enough to read, can barely hear the television (although she does enjoy watching it), and doesn't want to be bothered about voting because she feels she doesn't know enough about the candidates. She doesn't think it matters much. How will you convince her to go to the polls?

✳ Define the Problem

How do the rights and responsibilities of voting impact today's elections?
  or
Does the responsibility to vote override the right to vote or not to vote?
  or
How do we get Grandma to vote?
  or
What are the rights and responsibilities of the voter?
  or
Is the right to vote a privilege or a burden?

✳ Gather the Facts

Develop a KND chart or list (what we know, what we need to know, what we need to do).

What We Know

1. You have to be twenty-one to vote.
2. Blacks and women were given the right to vote later in the process.

**Problem-Based
Learning**

3. Not everyone exercises the right to vote.
4. More people are interested in a presidential election than in a non-presidential election.
5. There are groups that encourage voter registration and actual voting.
6. Politicians are represented through multimedia.
7. Some people vote based on their feelings rather than facts, data, and the politician's voting record.

What We Need to Know

1. How many people vote?
2. Who are they?
3. Why do these people vote?
4. How do advocate groups get people to vote?
5. How is the public informed about the candidates?
6. What form of media is most effective in informing the public?
7. What is the implication of the right *not* to vote?
8. How has the rights and responsibilities issue been defined and redefined over the years?
9. How can the elderly be encouraged to vote? African Americans? Women? Young people? Immigrants? Inner-city residents? Rural residents? Write-ins? Bed-ridden people?
10. Does my vote count?

What We Need to Do

1. Research past elections.
2. Take a survey of the elderly's opinions.
3. Investigate an advocate group.
4. Trace the history of the right to vote.
5. Hypothesize what might happen if the elderly were to no longer vote.
6. Create a campaign to get out the elderly vote.
7. Explore the issues of rights and responsibilities of voting.
8. Interview politicians running for office about their views.
9. Devise techniques to inform the elderly and infirm of the election issues and the candidates' qualifications.
10. Find out how many people on average voted in the last election; in the past five years; in the past decade; etc.
11. Discuss exactly what the constitution says about the rights and responsibilities of voting.

✳ Generate Questions

Based on the KND chart, compose questions that merit investigation. For example:

1. How many people vote?
2. Who are they?

3. What works? (Strategies to get different segments of society to vote.)

Without repeating all the information listed above in the KND chart, generate a new chart of questions that need to be addressed.

✳ Hypothesize

What if Grandma knew about the issues and the candidates? Would she be more inclined to vote?
> or

If the elderly were targeted by the media and by advocate groups with services, would they be more likely to vote?

✳ Research

The research cycle is continuous due to the students' findings from readings, interviews, surveys, current policy, and historical data. It is this intermittent pattern, the ebb and flow of findings that informs the problem. The information that emerges often suggests the next tier of investigation. For example, students researching advocate groups might first interview members who are activists. Then, as the students become aware of the advocate groups' missions, some may actually join a group and actively recruit voters. Since the students direct the flow and the intensity of the actual investigation, the activities vary accordingly.

✳ Rephrase the Problem

Refine the original statement.

How might the drive for voter participation target all segments of a society?
> or

Does every vote count, or do some votes count more than others?

✳ Generate Alternatives

Generate ideas and code them as probable, possible, or preferable. (The stakeholder in this case is the leader of a community group that advocates voters' responsibility to vote.)

1. The stakeholder keeps Grandma informed through regular conversations throughout the campaign and then arranges to take her to the polling place as part of a planned outing. (Possible)
2. The stakeholder creates an advocate group of young people to work toward informing the elderly and infirm about the election issues. (Preferable)
3. The stakeholder respects the wishes of Grandma and her right not to vote. (Probable)
4. The stakeholder convinces Grandma to vote and pursues the creation of an advocacy group to inform, encourage, and assist elderly voters. (Possible)

Problem-Based Learning

✳ Advocate Solutions

Based on the generated solutions and their coding, each student declares a preferable solution and justifies it with facts and feelings. For example:

Preferable Solution

Allow Grandma to decide for herself about whether or not to vote. At the same time, help her keep informed of the proceedings. Get involved in an advocacy group for voter participation.

Justification

The resolution respects the rights of individuals; expresses respect for elders; displays empathic understanding of another's viewpoint; and calls for future action on the part of the person concerned about the voting public.

MIDDLE SCHOOL EXAMPLE
Designer Genes

**Problem-Based
Learning**

✳ Meet the Problem

Geneticists today are able to locate particular genes and change their coding. While the scientific benefits are many in terms of eliminating genetic defects and undesirable hereditary traits for future generations, there are moral and ethical issues to consider: Who decides when to use genetic engineering? How are decisions made about genetic engineering? How is the process regulated to ensure human rights and individual rights? Consider the following scenario:

> You are the head of a team of scientists investigating genetic engineering. Your research is conclusive that a particular gene determines a predisposition to alcoholism.
>
> Brenda Moss is pregnant. Both she and her husband have a legacy of alcoholism that has devastated both of their families. While neither of them seem to be affected, through genetic counseling they have been cautioned about the possibilities of their children being alcoholics as well.
>
> They have been informed of the genetic team researching the problem and are considering becoming part of the study. The results of the genetic engineering, of course, will not be known for years. How might you convince them to allow your team to intervene?

✳ Define the Problem

How is genetic engineering beneficial to us?
> or

Are the results of genetic engineering worth the risks?
> or

What are the risks of genetic engineering?
> or

Is genetic engineering a viable option for pregnant women?
> or

How might Brenda and her husband make an informed decision?

✳ Gather the Facts

Use a KND chart or list (what we know, what we need to know, what we need to do).

What We Know

1. Genetic engineering is a reality.
2. The research on genetic engineering is long-term.

**Problem-Based
Learning**

3. Genetic engineers need to investigate all avenues of the research on genetic engineering.
4. There are many unknowns about genetic engineering.
5. There are moral and ethical issues that surface with the concept of genetic engineering.
6. We don't know much about genetic engineering. But, we know there is information about it on the Internet.

What We Need to Know

1. What is genetic engineering?
2. What are the risks? Benefits?
3. Who is researching this and where?
4. How much do scientists know about actual experimentation with humans?
5. What are the alternatives?
6. How do Brenda and her husband feel about the experiment?
7. What is the prognosis for success?
8. How critical is the decision for the health and well-being of the child?
9. What factors are most crucial to making a sound decision?

What We Need to Do

1. Research genetic engineering on the Internet and in the library.
2. Interview research scientists who know the facts.
3. Visit or write to an institution participating in genetic counseling.
4. Review the science-fiction literature for scenarios of genetic engineering.
5. Diagram the genetic information to understand recessive and dominant genes.
6. Gather data on studies completed.
7. Investigate alternatives.
8. Evaluate possible results.

✳ Generate Questions

Using the KND chart, revisit the information found and form questions for the investigation. For example:

1. What is genetic engineering?
2. How do we find out about genetic engineering?
3. Is there someone we can talk to?
4. Do we know how to find a genetic scientist on the Internet?

Without repeating all the information listed above in the KND chart, have students generate a new chart of questions that they need to address.

✳ Hypothesize

What if genetic engineering were better understood? Would that guide the decision?

> or

Is this a decision of the head or the heart?

> or

How might genetic engineering become a viable option?

Problem-Based Learning

✳ Research

The actual research data will vary depending on what questions drive the investigation, but the emerging information is certain to uncover future paths of interest. For example, as students think about the moral and ethical issues connected to genetic engineering, they might gather newspaper articles that highlight the issues and concerns families face with new technology. They might also accumulate personal interest stories on how families cope with genetic engineering and life-and-death decisions.

✳ Rephrase the Problem

Refine the original problem statement.

Is genetic engineering a reality for our families?

> or

What are the moral, ethical, and practical issues that surround the concept of genetic engineering?

> or

Will families elect to engineer the genetic structure of their children?

✳ Generate Alternatives

Generate ideas and code them as probable, possible, or preferable. (The stakeholder is the couple being asked to join the research study.)

1. Brenda and her husband opt to become part of the genetic team research. (Possible)
2. The couple reject the opportunity for genetic engineering. (Probable)
3. The family decides to continue to study about alcoholism and its prevention, but does not elect to be part of the research. (Preferable)

Problem-Based Learning

✳ Advocate Solutions

Based on the generated solutions and their coding, each student declares a preferable solution and justifies it with facts and feelings. For example:

Preferable Solution

The couple decides against genetic engineering, but pledges to each other to learn and understand about alcoholism.

Justification

While alcoholism is a possibility in their child's genetic makeup, the unknowns are too great to proceed as part of the research. If the genetic disorder were of critical proportions, such as mental retardation, perhaps the risk factors would be worth it. But, in this case, since some do not become affected with alcoholism even though they carry the gene, the decision to defer from the research study seems sound.

HIGH SCHOOL EXAMPLE
It's Out There!

✳ Meet the Problem

As part of a year-long curriculum effort to focus on the environment, a group of sixth grade teachers have asked a high school group to join forces with them to plan a comprehensive field experience. Consider the following scenario:

> You work as a student guide at a local ranch, which is often used with school groups. The possibilities for an outdoor education experience are endless. How will you lead your group in designing a comprehensive plan for the sixth graders that teachers, students, and parents will accept?

✳ Define the Problem

What kinds of outdoor experiences lead to understanding and appreciating the environment?

    or

Does outdoor education fit with an environmental focus in the curriculum?

    or

How does one design a comprehensive environmental experience?

    or

Can high-schoolers plan an environmentally rich experience for sixth graders?

✳ Gather the Facts

Develop a KND chart or list (what we know, what we need to know, what we need to do).

What We Know

1. Topics must include water, air, and land.
2. Activities must be safe.
3. Pollution might be a focus.
4. Living things include plants and animals.
5. Animal homes are interesting to study.
6. Identifying plants, trees, leaves, birds, tracks, and berries is fun.
7. Environmental issues are in the news every day.
8. Students respect the environment to varying degrees.
9. The life cycle is evidenced in the pond study.
10. Industry is often at odds with the environment.
11. The environment is at risk today.
12. People can do many things to save the earth.

**Problem-Based
Learning**

What We Need to Know

1. What time of year will the students have the outdoor experience?
2. What kind of weather can be expected?
3. What kinds of things have the students studied about the environment?
4. What do the students know about cloud formations? the ozone layer? water pollution? air pollution? noise pollution? life cycles? ecosystems?
5. How much can the students do on their own?
6. Do the students know how to research an idea?
7. What are the students interested in? Survival techniques? flora and fauna? tracking animals? bird watching?

What We Need to Do

1. Meet with the sixth grade teachers.
2. Survey the sixth-graders.
3. Look over the sixth grade texts.
4. Find out about environmental activities from the ranch staff.
5. Sketch out a rough draft and solicit feedback on it.
6. Research the climate, weather, and environment at a specified time of year.
7. Read about similar outdoor education programs.
8. Consider fundraising suggestions.
9. Possibly interview parents.
10. Gather materials, maps, brochures.
11. Make a brochure to sell the ranch idea.

✳ Generate Questions

Based on the KND chart, revisit the information and construct a list of questions that require investigation. For example:

1. What is a typical sixth grade curriculum?
2. What kinds of activities are appropriate?
3. Are sixth-graders held accountable for the experience?

Without repeating all the information listed above in the KND chart, generate a new chart of questions that need to be addressed.

✳ Hypothesize

What if a two- to four-day outdoor education experience could be planned around environmental issues? Would a brochure sell the idea?
> or

Why not have students from both schools work together to plan the experience?
> or

If the funding idea was accepted first, would the ranch idea sell more easily?

✳ Research

Through readings, surveys, interviews, and other research methods, the emerging information drives the project for the high school team. As the project evolves, the environmental unit takes shape, with adjustments along the way. Students might use the library, conduct interviews, or go online to search for information to form the problem. For example, students could visit the site of the outdoor education experience, survey the area, and delineate various venues for meaningful activities.

Problem-Based Learning

✳ Rephrase the Problem

Refine the original problem statement.

How might a high school team plan and implement an outdoor education program? ,
    or
What comprises an environmental unit for sixth-graders ?
    or
What environmental activities can enlighten young people about the environment?

✳ Generate Alternatives

Generate ideas and code them as probable, possible, or preferable. (The stakeholder in this case is the high school student in charge of planning.)
1. Design an environmental unit and present it to the teachers. (Probable)
2. Promote the idea of fundraising and an outdoor education experience at a ranch. (Possible)
3. Partner with the class and plan a relevant environmental unit. (Preferable)

✳ Advocate Solutions

Based on the generated solutions and their coding, each student declares a preferable solution and justifies it with facts and feelings. For example:

Preferable Solution

Orchestrate a cooperative effort in which the high school team works with the sixth grade to plan an environmental unit using the ranch as a plausible site.

Justification

The unit is bound to be more appropriately planned if the sixth-graders have a part in the planning. It is prudent to take advantage of an environmental site that is accessible and familiar.

**Problem-Based
Learning**

Where Is More Information?

Cognition and Curriculum Reconsidered by E. Eisner

Constructivism: Theory, Perspectives, and Practice by C. T. Fosnot

Developing Minds: A Resource Book for Teaching Thinking edited by A. Costa

Dimensions of Thinking by R. Marzano

Education and Learning to Think by L. Resnick

Education and the Creative Potential by E. P. Torrence

Experience and Education by J. Dewey

Guide to Creative Action by S. Parnes, R. Noller, and A. Biondi

How to Design a Problem-Based Learning Curriculum in the Pre-Clinical Years by H. Barrows

How to Solve It: A New Aspect of Mathematical Method by G. Polya

In Search of Understanding: The Case for the Constructivist Classroom by J. G. Brooks and M. G. Brooks

Instrumental Enrichment: An Intervention Program for Cognitive Modifiability by R. Feuerstein, Y. Rand., M. Hoffman, and R. Miller

Making Connections: Teaching and the Human Brain by G. Caine and R. N. Caine

Patterns for Thinking: Patterns for Transfer by R. Fogarty and J. Bellanca

Philosophy in the Classroom by M. Lipman, A. Sharp, and F. S. Oscanyan

Problem-Based Learning: A Multidisciplinary Approach (working title) by J. Barell

Schools for Talent Development: A Practical Plan for Total School Improvement by J. Renzulli

Teaching for Thoughtfulness: Classroom Strategies to Enhance Intellectual Development by J. Barell

Teaching Thinking by E. de Bono

The Mindful School: How to Teach for Metacognitive Reflection by R. Fogarty

The Mindful School: How to Teach for Transfer by R. Fogarty, D. Perkins, and J. Barell

The Teaching of Thinking by R. Nickerson, D. Perkins, and E. Smith

Toward a Coherent Curriculum by J. Beane

IRI/SkyLight Training and Publishing

What's My Thinking Now?

Reflections:

....
....
....
....
....
....
....

Questions:

....
....
....
....
....
....
....
....

Comments:

....
....
....
....
....
....
....

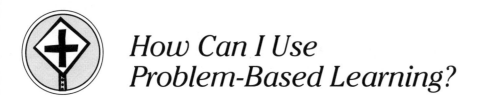

How Can I Use Problem-Based Learning?

Use this outline to apply problem-based learning to your content and classroom.

✳ **Meet the Problem** (Sketch out a scenario of a relevant issue.)

....
....
....
....
....
....
....

✳ **Define the Problem** (Try to summarize the problem.)

....
....
....
....
....
....
....
....

✳ **Gather the Facts** (Draw a KND chart.)

What We **K**now	What We **N**eed to Know	What We Need to **D**o

How Can I Use Problem-Based Learning?

✳ **Generate Questions** (Use the KND chart to generate relevant questions.)

....
....
....
....
....
....
....

✳ **Hypothesize** (Predict possible paths to investigate.)

....
....
....
....
....
....
....

✳ **Research** (Read, interview, surf the Internet, visit a site.)

....
....
....
....
....
....
....

How Can I Use Problem-Based Learning?

✳ **Rephrase the Problem** (Refine the original problem statement.)

....
....
....
....
....
....
....
....

✳ **Generate Alternatives** (Select probable, possible, and preferable solutions.)

....
....
....
....
....
....
....
....

✳ **Advocate Solutions** (Choose a solution and justify it.)

....
....
....
....
....
....
....

IRI/SkyLight Training and Publishing

CASE
STUDIES

Examine the contents, not the bottle.
—Talmud

Case Studies

What Are Case Studies?

Case studies are detailed accounts of specific situations. They extrapolate core issues and inherent beliefs about how each of us views and values our world. Well-structured cases offer ambiguity, dilemmas, paradoxes, problems to solve, and decisions to make. Students think through these cases using structured discussions and Socratic dialogue—forms of higher-order thinking processes.

In an effort to present learning within a contextual framework that provides relevant meaning, case studies are designed to provoke deep understanding. Case studies cause students to infer, generalize, and draw conclusions while grappling with authentic situations and the ramifications. They illuminate learning by presenting slice-of-life scenarios that require complex interactions to unravel.

What Do Case Studies Look and Sound Like?

Cases that are appropriately selected, phrased, and conducted can target learners from young to adult. A case study may involve a moral dilemma, such as whether or not it is right to lie if it is an act of kindness; a paradoxical situation, such as a scenario in which a coward becomes a hero at a crucial moment, begging the question of whether or not the person is truly heroic; or a situation concerning business ethics, such as fair and honest tax practices. Of course, the ideas mentioned here are thoroughly developed in the studies. In each case, a vignette provides fodder for further investigation. Once the scenario is exposed, a process for studying the case begins. Following is an example of a case scenario.

A Question for Friends

Betsy and Jamie are best friends. They're fifteen and they've been buddies since kindergarten. They do everything together, including after-school ice-skating classes, hanging out, and, of course, homework. Their other friends know that they are inseparable. Where one goes, the other goes too.

As part of their summer plans, the two enrolled in a summer skating camp. When they arrived at the camp, they realized they had been assigned to different rooms and weren't scheduled to be roommates. They immediately appealed to the director, citing their close friendship and expectations of being together. Former policy ruled and they were sent back to their dorm.

Angry and frustrated by the decision, the two manufactured a story for their unsuspecting roommates. In short order, they entered Betsy's room and told the new girl, Cory, that there had been a mistake. They told her she had really been assigned to the room down the hall. Feeling somewhat flustered and left out of this impenetrable circle created by Betsy and Jamie, Cory scrambled to unmake her bunk and quickly gather her things.

As she attempted to drag her stuff down the hall, Betsy and Jamie enthusiastically volunteered to give her a hand. When Cory found the room, Betsy and Jamie made up a lame excuse to leave and ran back to "their" room. Tumbling onto the beds, they giggled and "high-fived" each other, exclaiming, "After all, what are friends for?"

A vignette provides a platform for further investigation of a case. It provokes students to engage in rigorous discussions about the implications of the characters' actions while examining the issues and pursuing the case according to the guidelines that govern it. An appropriately selected, phrased, and conducted case may target varying ages of learners, from very young students to adult learners.

How Do Case Studies Work?

According to Wasserman (1991), the key elements of a case study are the following:

1. A compelling narrative rooted in the key issues of the curriculum
2. A narrative summary of the facts

3. Small group discussions sparked by thought-provoking questions
4. Teacher-led debriefing sessions that encourage reasoning from the data
5. Follow-up readings and research for more extensive examination

In addition to these key elements, the case studies in this book are enriched by a multiple intelligences approach. Let's look more closely at each of the components and how they unfold in a case study.

Case Studies

✳ Compelling Narrative

The narrative is based on big ideas, central issues, and conceptual understandings that are targeted in the curriculum areas (history, economics, government, and bioethics). The narrative is written as a real-life problem, making it inherently interdisciplinary. It doesn't end with an explicit or even an implied resolution. Rather, it sets up an ambiguous situation—a dilemma that encourages debate, reflection, and the need to know more.

Several intelligences can be identified in the case study model. The extensive use of the verbal/linguistic intelligence is evident, but the visual/spatial and the interpersonal intelligences also come into play as students imagine the scenario and empathize with the people involved.

✳ Facts

Present a narrative summary statement of the facts before the small group discussions begin. The summary provides a focus for the discussion as well as relevant information for the investigation. It is a step in the process that dictates a clear synthesis.

✳ Small Group Discussions

Small group discussions involve students in groups of three to five. The discussions revolve around a set of questions structured by the teacher-leader. While the questions may be carefully tailored to the particular case at hand, according to Wasserman (1994), they (1) always require thoughtful examination of the facts; (2) are keyed to the big ideas; (3) invite, rather than command; and (4) are sequenced in some logical progression that taps into the logical intelligence. For example, the questions usually begin with a call for the students to identify, in their opinion, what the "central issues" are in the case. Then, the students are asked to imagine or draw a verbal picture of the scenario in as much detail as possible. Students then immerse themselves in the situation and empathize with the people in the story. In turn, the students generalize their statements. Following are examples of tailored instructions used to guide a small group discussion:

1. Discern the significant issues.
2. Create a verbal picture.

3. Describe what this situation might be like.
4. Compare this situation to a current situation.
5. Agree or disagree with key points of the situation.
6. Explain how this situation might be handled differently.
7. Justify the reason for handling the situation described.
8. Draw a similar example from your personal experience.

Students can also be asked to respond to a generic set of questions that seem appropriate to any scenario. These questions might follow the format one teacher uses in his religious studies classes at Santa Marguarita High School (1995). The following generic questions address the verbal/linguistic, logical/mathematical, interpersonal, intrapersonal, bodily/kinesthetic (experiential), and visual/spatial:

1. Citing the facts, what do you conclude are the key issues?
2. What do you imagine as possible actions and consequences?
3. Seeking insight beyond your own, what do you infer?
4. Turning inward, how do you assess your own values?
5. Generalizing your beliefs, yet based on the facts presented, what is your decision and how do you justify it?

These examples of teacher-led questions provoke student thinking about the case. When first using case studies, they provide structure and appropriateness. However, original questions tailored to the particular cases are usually most effective.

✳ Debriefing

The debriefing process gives students an opportunity to articulate their understandings. They also infer from facts, examine their assumptions, and evaluate inconsistencies and differences in points of view. Debriefing is a critical component of the case study. The teacher's artful questioning and responding help students reason from the data and assume responsibility for their ideas.

Debriefing sessions move from big ideas and central issues to specific facts and data that support and justify generalizations. A key strategy for teacher-leaders is to paraphrase and echo ideas voiced by students. In this way, students have keen opportunities to examine what they say within a new framework. Developed by Wasserman (1994), debriefing sessions are open-discussion formats in which the teacher refrains from interjecting his or her own thoughts. Instead, the teacher prods the students to think about the situation.

Once students have studied the case, teachers assess the students' understanding of its key issues. Teachers ask the students what their opinions are about the case. This is the time when further development through probing questions and in-depth discussions about personal values might be necessary, based on the reactions the teacher receives.

**Case
Studies**

It is not necessary for all students to agree or reach consensus. The purpose of the debriefing is to help students grasp the complexity of the issues. In fact, students are encouraged to think for themselves and to debate the dilemmas and contradictions of the case. The supreme lesson in all cases is that there are no easy answers to many of the questions in life—issues can become complicated by the values one holds dear.

Debriefing sessions reveal the ambiguity in key issues that we all face. They focus students on how they might think through similar or parallel cases, which they will undoubtedly encounter in the future. For example, the following ideas might provide more clarity and insight: define, compare, defend, generalize, give personal examples, hypothesize, summarize, and use analogies.

✳ Follow-Up

Follow-up activities invite further investigation into case studies. They invite interdisciplinary work, just as real-life situations reach out to various disciplines in search of additional data and needed information. For example, as students seek to learn more about the case and/or the key issues related to the case, they follow myriad leads. Their search may take them to the Internet to find information related to the case study; call on their language skills to interview experts; or push them into history for background material. Obviously, as students integrate various disciplines, they also interweave multiple intelligences into their learning. In particular, they may be required to prepare multidimensional presentations that call on several intelligences.

Follow-up activities are done individually, in pairs, or in small groups. In fact, the follow-up activity may even become part of the class work, incorporated into a whole group venture. Of course, whatever follow-up activities are used, their content and context must eventually be integrated into the group discussions. The students need to know additional information to make informed decisions. Therefore, the new findings must become an integral part of the case.

Who Are the Key Players and What Are Their Roles?

Teachers

The teacher's role is absolutely critical to a case study, because the teacher frames the case, poses the questions, encourages thoughtful discussion, listens to the responses, and continues to provoke deep learning throughout the case study. Using skillful Socratic questioning techniques (Lipman, Sharp, and Oscanyan 1980), the teacher ensures that the fullest learning potential is derived from the case. The teacher fuels the investigation through the power of questioning, uncovering the subtleties and intricacies of the complex life issues that emerge.

Students

Students also play crucial roles in case studies. They are the investigators. They are seeking information on the case in order to make mindful decisions and determine sensible solutions. In fact, students are the protagonists in case study scenarios. They immerse themselves in situations in order to make decisions that are not only informed, but that also reflect their own values and beliefs. The case study, because of its personalized nature, affords students many opportunities to dive into the middle of the muddle. From a personal perspective, students are able to easily experience the actions and feelings of the people involved. Thus, they are more able to respond empathically, which is an important goal of the case study model.

Case Studies

Why Do Case Studies Work?

Using qualitative research methodologies (Miles and Huberman 1984) and field study techniques (Isaac and Michael 1981) of ethnographic research, the case study model evolves. It is geared to issues that are relevant to young people. Thus, instead of studying other cultures or historic civilizations, the case study method in this publication deals with issues that directly impact students today.

Mathew Lipman (1980) has developed a comprehensive series of books on philosophy for children that uses the case study method to present moral dilemmas. Sylvia Wasserman (1994) is another advocate of the case study method. Through her case studies depicting teachers in the "art of teaching," Wasserman demonstrates how case studies can be used in preservice and inservice models to study teaching. Phil Hallinger (1993), at Vanderbilt University, illustrates the use of case studies in his work with administrators and school leaders. Elliot Eisner (1985) embraces the case study method in his efforts in educational evaluation.

With the rich history of the case study as a method aligned with rigorous pedagogical theory, it seems natural that it has become a model for the classroom in this period of intense interest in integrated models and authentic learning. As schools revisit traditional practices and move toward more learner-centered models such as block scheduling and year-round schooling, larger chunks of time are carved out of the school day and the school year to allow for models of learning that shepherd deep understanding. The case study is such a model.

Case Studies

When Can Case Studies Be Used Effectively?

ELEMENTARY EXAMPLE
"You're Not the Boss of Me!"

✳ Key Concepts

authority, responsibility, independence, loyalty, democracy

✳ Content and/or Disciplines

government, speech, history, politics

✳ Compelling Narrative

"You're not the boss of me!" Shenelle shouted as she slammed her locker door and abruptly turned away from her sister, Lorna. "Stop trying to run my life. I'm old enough to make my own decisions."

"No, you're not," Lorna retorted. "That's obvious by the one you just made. You know darn well Mom and Dad won't approve of your cutting class, regardless of how noble you think your reason is."

"We only elect a president every four years. It would be stupid not to take advantage of this opportunity. How many times does a presidential candidate campaign in your own hometown? I'm going to the rally with my friends and you should go too. You're gonna be sorry if you don't."

"You're the one who is going to live to regret this. Wait 'til Mom and Dad find out. And they *will* find out. You can count on that."

"Are you gonna tell?"

"I have to. When they find out, they're gonna ask me if I knew. I'm not getting in trouble just because you've been hit with a dose of pseudo-patriotism. Just grow up, will you. Do the right thing for a change."

"It is the right thing."

✳ Facts

A presidential candidate is campaigning in Shenelle's hometown; her friends are cutting school to attend the rally; she has decided to go; her sister, Lorna, objects; Lorna plans to tell their parents; the sisters are fighting about who is the boss in this situation.

✳ Small Group Discussions (3–5 Students)

1. Why is Lorna so upset?
2. Do both sisters have responsibility for Shenelle's actions?

3. Do you agree or disagree with Shenelle's statement that "it would be stupid not to take advantage of the opportunity"?
4. What role does the school play in this case?
5. Is Lorna the boss of Shenelle?
6. Can both sisters be doing the right thing?
7. Compare the sisters' rights and responsibilities to situations in your lives.
8. How might each sister have handled the situation differently?
9. Agree or disagree with one of the sisters.

**Case
Studies**

✳ Debriefing (Whole Group)

1. Paraphrase the key points.
2. What else seems significant?
3. Tell us more about that.
4. Anchor that idea with an example.
5. What generalizations are we ready to make?
6. What are the various viewpoints that you feel comfortable defending?
7. Predict similar situations you may encounter in the future and justify your anticipated actions.

✳ Follow-Up

Knowing the authority issues that arise for middle-schoolers, role-plays may help them think through appropriate reactions. Use some of the following role-plays:

1. Siblings
2. Teacher/student
3. Babysitter/child
4. Teenager/elder
5. Police/citizen
6. Student/substitute teacher
7. Principal/student
8. Teenager/older friend

Case Studies

MIDDLE SCHOOL EXAMPLE
A Lie Is a Lie Is a Lie

✳ Key Concepts

truth, integrity, honesty

✳ Content and/or Disciplines

social studies, psychology, adviser/advisee

✳ Compelling Narrative

"I love your outfit, Sue!" said Ann.

"Have you ever seen anything so ugly?" Ann whispered to Beth as they walked past Sue. "It makes her look like a two-ton Tony."

"If you really think it's that bad, why did you compliment Sue? Why not just say nothing at all?"

"Beth, if it makes her feel better, who cares?"

"I care, Ann! I think it's insincere and phony. In fact, it's really like telling a lie!"

"Be serious. How can saying something nice to someone be as wrong as telling a real lie? If I lie to my parents about my homework, that's a lie. But if I make someone happy by saying something that is not totally true, that's not the same."

"I've gotta go. I'll call you later, after I visit my grandma at the nursing home."

"OK. See ya later."

   🙐 🙐 🙐

Later that evening, Beth called Ann.

"Hi, Ann. What are you doing?"

"I'm just doing my algebra. What a drag. How's your grandma?"

"Oh, she's not doing very well. The doctors have discovered more cancer and there's nothing they can do. It makes me so sad to see her like this. But, at least she doesn't know how bad it really is. They're not gonna tell her everything. There's no reason to."

"If it were me, I'd want to know. It's kinda like lying if they know something and don't say what they know."

"Oh, great, here we go again with the 'is-it-a-lie-or-isn't-it-a-lie?' bit. I just called to talk because I was feeling down in the dumps about Gramma. I don't want to get into this whole thing again. I'll see ya tomorrow. Bye."

✳ Facts

Ann tells her friend Sue that she likes her outfit. Then she confides to Beth that the outfit is really not flattering at all. Beth accuses Ann of "lying" because she said something insincere. Later, Ann turns the tables and tells Beth that it's a "lie" to withhold information from her grandmother about her grandmother's cancer.

✳ Small Group Discussions (3–5 Students)

1. Describe the first scene between Ann and Beth.
2. Describe a time when you did something similar.
3. How was Beth's response similar to or different from your thinking?
4. How might Beth have responded to Ann?
5. Is Beth's situation different from Ann's? Why or why not?
6. Rank the following from one to four, four being the worst: __lie, __white lie, __misstatement, __withholding information. Justify your rankings.
7. Agree or disagree with the following statements:
   • Ann did not really lie about Sue's outfit.
   • The family did not really lie about Gramma.

✳ Debriefing (Whole Group)

1. Generalize your thoughts about lies.
2. Paraphrase the point Ann made about her parents and homework.
3. What seems most significant in the scenario between Ann and Beth? Why?
4. Create a scenario in which the truth is withheld, misrepresented, or distorted. Justify the situation.
5. Predict what might happen next between Ann and Beth.
6. Defend a particular point of view concerning when a statement or situation is a lie and when it isn't. Use supporting details.

✳ Follow-Up

• Survey other students for their thinking on what a lie is. Ask them if they think a lie can be justified.
• Find examples of different types of lying in literature, film, and video.
• Look up the definition of "lie" in several dictionaries. Find and define euphemisms for lying and give your opinion of your findings.

**Case
Studies**

HIGH SCHOOL EXAMPLE
Who Says?

✳ **Key Concepts**

censorship, bias, individual rights

✳ **Content and/or Disciplines**

social studies, government, art, media, graphic arts, literature

✳ **Compelling Narrative**

"I can't believe the movie that was on last night during prime time viewing," Jan told her friend Jo. "It's a disgrace to our society that they would show that filth on television. Someone has to get control of this."

"I agree," Jo responded. "But I'm not sure how much control I would want. Do you mean a rating system such as they use in the film industry? That might be acceptable to me, but I have concerns about any real censorship."

"I think a rating system is absolutely necessary. In fact, I'd rather have the government control it rather than letting the networks create their own rating system. I think a government agency might be less likely to be influenced by personal interest groups."

"Government regulation seems too much like real censorship—'Big Brother' is watching, and all that stuff. Next thing you know, we'll have them burning our books. No, I think I prefer to leave TV viewing to the discretion of the parents or the family. I think I value my right to choose over the government's responsibility to protect."

"Listen to what you're saying. You'd actually compare a rating system to real censorship. It's simply a code for the public to be aware of. You would still have the choice to watch or not to watch."

"I'm just afraid that if we open the door to censorship of the airwaves, there will be no end to it. Look at the headlines, they're already talking about V-chips and regulation of the Internet."

"Oh, Jo, you're making too much of this. I'm talking about a simple rating system, similar to what already exists for movie-goers. It works. People have some idea of what they're going to see."

"I know. But regulation of television, or even the Internet, is different. These are in our homes."

"No kidding. That's just the point. Don't you want control of what comes into your own home?"

"Yes, that's exactly right, Jen. I want to decide for myself. I don't want someone else to decide for me."

"Oh, I give up. We're saying the same thing. Let's just drop it for now."

✳ Facts

Film ratings are based on predetermined standards; television and the Internet are not rated for violence/explicit sex; Jen suggests a similar rating system for TV and maybe for the Internet; Jo opposes government intervention and/or any regulation or censorship.

**Case
Studies**

✳ Small Group Discussions (3–5 Students)

1. Are Jen and Jo saying the same thing?
2. Clarify the issue of a rating system.
3. Compare a rating system to censorship.
4. Agree or disagree with the following statement: Censorship is a necessary evil.
5. Rank the following according to their role in regulating television viewing: individual, government, network.
6. Determine what the standards are and apply them to television programming.
7. Describe a personal experience in which censorship became an issue.

✳ Debriefing (Whole Group)

1. Define censorship, standards, rating system, regulation, individual rights, responsibility.
2. Compare parent regulation with government regulation.
3. Defend your thinking about individual rights vs. government regulation.
4. Give personal examples that deal with the issue of who decides.
5. Generalize your thinking on censorship issues.
6. Hypothesize a situation in which you feel censorship goes too far.
7. Summarize the issues that are relevant to you and tell why they are relevant.
8. Anchor your thinking about outside controls and individual rights with real-life examples from the news.

✳ Follow-Up

- Investigate the film industry rating system. Who sets the standards? Who really decides the rating? How has it affected the film industry? Benefits? Detriments?
- Describe how the V-chip works and agree or disagree with the idea. Support your opinions with facts.
- Trace the historical context of the term "Big Brother."
- Research the censorship issue in terms of its effect on libraries throughout the states.
- Use the Internet to track issues of censorship.
- Develop a campaign either for or against censorship.

**Case
Studies**

Where Is More Information?

Art As Experience by J. Dewey

The Birth of Logical Thinking from Childhood to Adolescence by J. Piaget

Cases for Teaching in the Secondary School by S. Wasserman

The Child's Conception of the World by J. Piaget

Cognitive Perspective on Educational Leadership by P. Hallinger, K. Leithwood, and J. Murphy

Contemporary Aesthetics by M. Lipman

Discovering Philosophy by M. Lipman

Educational Imagination: On the Design and Evaluation of School Programs by E. Eisner

Educational Judgements by J. Doyle

Ethical Inquiry: Instructional Manual to Accompany Lisa by M. Lipman, A. M. Sharp, and F. S. Oscanyan

Growing Up with Philosophy by M. Lipman and A. M. Sharp

Handbook in Research and Evaluation: For Education and the Behavioral Sciences by S. Isaac and W. Michael

Harry Stottlemeier's Discovery by M. Lipman

An Introduction to Logic and Scientific Method by M. Cohen and E. Nagel

Judgment and Reasoning in the Child by J. Piaget

Lisa by M. Lipman

Logic in Teaching by R. Ennis

Logic: The Theory of Inquiry by J. Dewey

Mark by M. Lipman

Philosophy in the Classroom by M. Lipman, A. M. Sharp, and F. S. Oscanyan

Qualitative Data Analysis: A Sourcebook of New Methods by M. Miles and A. M. Huberman

Suki by M. Lipman

"Teaching and Learning Beyond the Text" by C. M. Fairbanks in *Journal of Curriculum and Supervision,* September 1994

Teaching As a Subversive Activity by N. Postman and C. Weingartner

Teaching for Thinking by L. E. Raths et al.

The Theory of the Moral Life by J. Dewey

"Using Cases to Study Teaching" by S. Wasserman in *Phi Delta Kappan,* April 1994

What Happens in Art by M. Lipman

"What Is a Discussion?" by J. Buchler in *Journal of General Education,* October 1954

What's My Thinking Now?

Reflections:

....
....
....
....
....
....
....

Questions:

....
....
....
....
....
....
....

Comments:

....
....
....
....
....
....
....

How Can I Use Case Studies?

Use this outline to apply case studies to your content and classroom.

✳ **Key Concepts**

....
....
....

✳ **Content and/or Disciplines**

....
....
....

✳ **Compelling Narrative** (Outline a big idea for a narrative.)

....
....
....
....
....
....
....
....
....

✳ **Facts** (Summarize the facts from the narrative.)

....
....
....
....
....
....
....
....
....

How Can I Use Case Studies?

✴ **Small Group Discussions** (Generate questions—discern, create, describe, compare, agree/disagree, explain, justify.)

....
....
....
....
....
....
....
....
....

✴ **Debriefing** (Pose questions to synthesize—defend, generalize, hypothesize, give personal examples.)

....
....
....
....
....
....
....
....
....

How Can I Use Case Studies?

✱ **Follow-Up** (Create a list of related experiences.)

....
....
....
....
....
....
....
....
....
....
....
....
....
....
....
....
....
....

THEMATIC
LEARNING

An idea is a feat of association.
—Robert Frost

Thematic Learning

What Is a Theme?

Themes are big ideas that provide organizing centers for curriculum development and ignite learning for students. Used as an umbrella idea, the theme spreads out to various disciplines or subject matter content. Themes, or "big ideas," such as "friendship," "exploration," or "intelligence" are unifying elements that integrate the disciplines in relevant, authentic, and purposeful ways.

For example, think about a science unit on the human body in which students learn about the circulatory *system,* digestive *system,* skeletal *system,* and all other bodily *systems*. Then, imagine the conceptual shift that occurs when students encounter *systems* of transportation in social studies, computer *systems* in tech prep class, the Dewey decimal *system* in the library, or a discussion of the school *system* at the dinner table. Imagine how much bigger the idea of *systems* becomes to students as they transfer the idea across the disciplines and into their lives.

What Does a Theme Look and Sound Like?

Thematic learning in the classroom consists of learning activities and experiences that connect subject matter from different disciplines. The units may involve two disciplines working in harmony (for instance, a unit in literature can tie into a history class). A theme can also connect five or six disciplines. For example, an umbrella unit on the Olympics can incorporate physical education, language arts, art, math, science, and social studies. Activities can be planned so that the six areas all connect.

The P.E. curriculum of sports, games, fitness, teamwork, and competition fit perfectly with the theme of the Olympics. Greek mythology and universal concepts such as pride, accomplishment, endurance, and inter- and intrapersonal skills are all relevant to physical education. Students can read biographies and historical fiction and write about the Olympics in language arts. In addition, students can study ancient architectural forms, pottery, paintings, modern-day poster art, and computer graphics of the events. The connections for math are also limitless: data gathering, statistical analysis, and logic can be used to make predictions about the events. Physics, chemistry, and biology provide opportunities for students to learn about the athletic events, training techniques, and equipment designs of the Olympics. Finally, Greek history and geographic and regional studies fit easily under this Olympic umbrella.

Themes provide visible connections not only to different areas of study, but also to different intelligences. The multiple intelligences (Gardner 1983) are a part of all of the activities just mentioned, providing a variety of ways for students to experience them. (For a summary of the multiple intelligences theory, refer to the Introduction. There are also reference charts on pages xx–xxii.)

Following are a subject matter web (fig. 3.1) and a multiple intelligences grid (fig. 3.2) of activities based on the same theme. Compare the two and use the one best suited to your teaching situation. Or, more specifically, use the web of activities to survey some initial ideas or to plan a brief unit of study on the Olympics. The grid of activities presents multiple opportunities for a more comprehensive unit of study that spans a greater period of time than the web activities. The Olympic web might include a week-long focus, while the grid may require several weeks to complete.

Thematic Learning

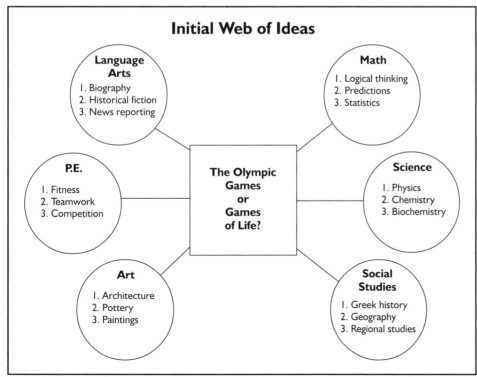

Figure 3.1

Thematic Learning

The multiple intelligences grid of activities presents the skeletal structure of possible learning experiences extrapolated from the Olympic Games theme. In each of the columns, one of Gardner's intelligences is targeted and appropriate areas of study are indicated. The grid of ideas is evidence of the multidimensional options the theme provides.

Multiple Intelligences Grid of Ideas
The Olympic Games or Games of Life

Visual	Verbal	Logical	Musical	Bodily	Interpersonal	Intrapersonal	Naturalist
Greek architecture	Biographies	Graphic arts	National songs	Fitness	Teamwork	Individual achievement	Nutrition
Pottery	Writing about heroes	Biochemistry	Races	Sports	Cooperation	Pride	Health
Paintings	Historical fiction	Laws of physics	Practicing music	Practice	Competition	Sense of accomplishment	Wellness
Posters	Myths	Statistics	Relaxation music	Routines	Sportsmanship		Biochemistry
Photos	Literature	Percentages	Meditation	Regimens	Coaching	Logs	Climate
Graphic organizers	News reporting	Logical thinking	Composing	Physical therapy	Mentoring	Journals	Culture
Graphs	Expository writing	Sequences	Performing	Conditioning	Global relationships	Psychology of peak performance	Biofeedback
Visualization techniques	Features	Cause/effect	Selecting appropriate music	Experiences	Conflict management	Endurance	Altitudes

Figure 3.2

IRI/SkyLight Training and Publishing

How Do Themes Work?

The three steps to developing a thematic unit are brainstorming, posing questions about the theme, and turning the theme into an investigation.

✳ Brainstorming a Bank of Themes

The most critical step in developing a thematic unit is the initial brainstorming of themes. Generating ideas to create a bank of candidate themes can be done in a relatively short amount of time. They can be brainstormed by (1) listing general ideas, and (2) listing ideas by categories.

Listing general ideas begins by recalling themes the group has read about, heard about, or discovered in the content they teach. To enhance this teacher-generated list of ideas, students can also develop their own bank of themes. The two lists together offer a unique opportunity to compare, combine, and adapt in an attempt to select themes of relevance and student interest.

Teacher-Generated List

Habits of Mind	Justice	People
Rights of Passage	Bridges	Animals
The Global Village	Walls	Structures
The Environment	Rain Forests	Beauty
Outer Space	Dinosaurs	Friendship
Travel	Growing	Decades
The Farm	Mysteries	Transportation

Student-Generated List

Justice	Communication	Ecology
Rights	Family	Careers
Responsibility	Wild Things	Technology
Famous People	Heritage	Legends
The Ocean	Flying	The Future

**Thematic
Learning**

The second type of brainstorm involves a defined method for generating theme ideas. By targeting specific categories of ideas, themes emerge in a variety of genres. For example, themes slotted under the following labels yield an abundance of ideas in eight different areas: topics, concepts, problems, films, novels, songs, upcoming school or community events, and a "miscellaneous" or "other" category that serves as a catch-all.

Topics: Plants, living things, solar system, World War II, dreams, bridges

Concepts: Equality, power, vision, interdependence, honesty, courage

Problems: Violence, poverty, homelessness, aggression, ecology, war

Films: *The Great Gatsby, Journey to the Center of the Earth, Babe*

Novels: *Gone with the Wind, Of Mice and Men, Huckleberry Finn*

Songs: "The Sound of Music," "The Farmer in the Dell," "Imagine"

Events: Earth day, zoo trip, outdoor education week, parent night

Miscellaneous: Habits, world of work, grandparents, cultures

✳ Posing Questions

Traditional themes, such as *Canada,* the *environment, dinosaurs,* and *rain forests,* are both broadened and deepened when driven by questions. Questions create an atmosphere of inquiry and lead to a unit of study that becomes an investigation. For example, the rain forest theme shifts from a topic in social studies to a conceptual theme of a universal nature when one asks, "How is the rain forest a reign of life?" The rain forest now becomes a platform for learning about living things and their life cycles. "Bridges: What Do They Connect?" is another theme that poses a question which opens the way for activities with real bridges and topics. It also addresses the ideas of emotional bridges and bridges as transitions. Students find that there are many concepts behind the idea of bridges.

By using the same brainstorming technique used to produce an initial list of themes, a group can expound on any given theme. Group members begin by asking questions that relate to the theme, letting the questions flow for several minutes and piggybacking on one another's ideas. It is important to ask students questions that force them to address the theme's critical issues. The theme then branches out in several directions while narrowing in focus. For example, the world is explored in the following list of questions. Notice how open-ended the listing becomes.

Theme: The World

1. Who rules the world?
2. What is the world economy?
3. How is the world shrinking?
4. Is this the only world?
5. How do I fit in this world? (Key Question)
6. What can I do to make this a better world?
7. What does a world view look like?
8. Are we the world?
9. How are we the world? (Key Question)
10. Can I stop the world and get off?
11. How worldly am I?
12. Who has flown around the world?
13. Does it take eighty days to fly around the world?
14. Is the world a person, place, or thing? (Key Question)
15. When will the world end? How? Why?
16. What are bridges to other worlds? (Key Question)

Thematic Learning

Look for a key question in the list of questions. It should be a hook for the students, a question that has some cleverness, wit, humor, or a double meaning. It should be "genius" level, but not stuffy like the questions that appear at the end of textbook chapters. The key, or "hook," question must have kid appeal, as it will become a refrain that students repeat throughout the thematic unit. The following examples suggest how powerful a hook question can be.

Relationships—Making Them or Breaking Them?

Violence—Can We Kill It?

Bridges—What Do They Bridge?

Seeds—Is It the Seed of an Idea?

Systems—Open or Closed?

Bridges—What Are the Connections?

**Thematic
Learning**

The hook question may be more of a statement than a question. For example, the following themes are served best with a hook statement rather than a question:

> Space: An Odyssey
>
> Wonder: The Key to Learning
>
> History: Lessons from the Past
>
> The Magic of Numbers
>
> Living Things: The Miracle of Life
>
> Architecture: Building a Legacy
>
> Information Highway: Show Me the Way
>
> Music on My Mind

✳ Turning a Theme into a Problem-Solving Investigation

Posing questions about a theme can turn the thematic unit into a problem(s) to ponder, manipulate, and investigate. Questions can lead directly to a problem-solving approach that guides the students' work with a theme. A refined theme formed around questions (or statements) can take on a universal perspective. It can present open-ended and diverse themes such as "Bridges: What Are the Connections?" This theme leads to myriad possibilities for investigation: Do bridges connect bodies of land only, or do they connect cultures, people, and ideas too? What kind of bridges connect cultures? How do we build those bridges? What happens when the bridges break down? Aren't there poetic bridges in literature? romantic bridges in history? theoretical bridges in mathematical thinking? genetic bridges in biology? human bridges in psychology? and structural bridges in architecture? These big ideas are problematic in nature and present universal dilemmas.

Figure 3.3 is an example of a web that illustrates ideas for the bridges theme. This web suggests possible discipline-based learning experiences that relate to the big idea. In addition, figure 3.4 presents a grid of ideas for the bridges theme. These ideas are framed around the multiple intelligences. Review these graphic organizers to see how the bridges theme involves several disciplines and intelligences.

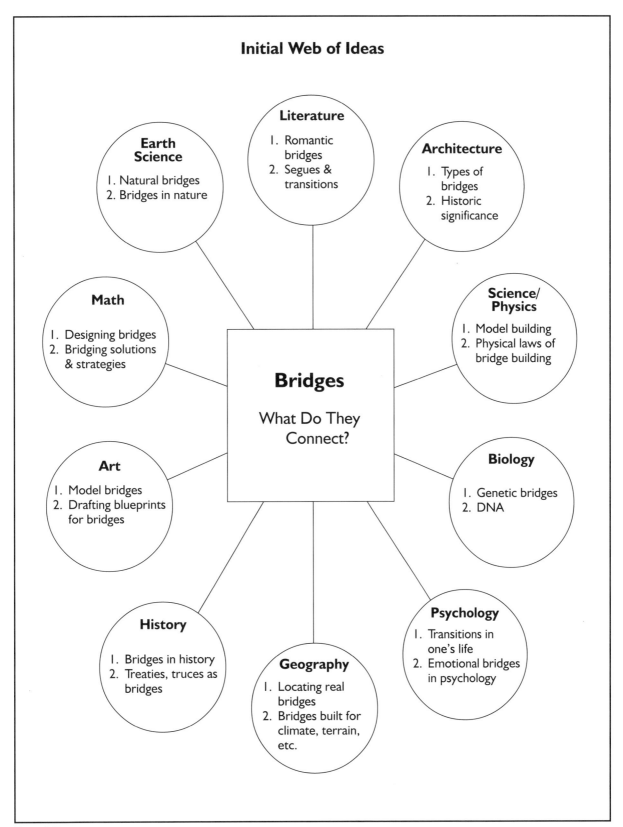

Figure 3.3

Multiple Intelligences Grid of Ideas
Bridges: What Do They Connect?

Visual
- Films (*Bridge Over the River Kwai*)
- Drafting
- Blueprints
- Flow chart
- Images
- Covered bridges
- Drawing bridges
- Cartoons w/bridges
- Comics w/bridges
- Painting/sketching bridges
- Calendar of bridges

Verbal
- Poetry
- Transitions
- Segues
- Literature about bridges or bridges in titles (*Bridges of Madison County*)
- Descriptive writing
- Expository writing
- Transitional language
- Prepositional phrases
- Romantic bridges (figurative)

Logical
- Stress analysis
- Physics of strength
- Geometric laws
- Building working models
- Scale drawings
- Bridging solutions
- Political bridges (ambassadors, diplomats)
- Economic bridges (NAFTA, Open Skies)
- Statistical bridges

Musical
- Songs w/bridges in lyrics
- Composing songs about bridges
- Selecting music to represent various types of bridges
- Music that bridges the decades, or eras, or nations

Bodily
- Sculpting bridges
- Building models
- Human bridges (circle of friends)
- Bridges in sports (Bungee jumping)
- Crossing bridges
- Physiological bridges (skeletal system, muscular system)
- Field trips
- Excursions

Interpersonal
- Relationships as bridges
- Bridges to past (grandparents)
- Bridges to future (babies)
- Emotional bridges (tolerance)
- Psychological bridges (coping strategies)
- Bridging the generation gap
- Bridging ages & phases of life (life passages)

Intrapersonal
- Bridging from one stage to the next
- Meditations as bridges to self
- Personal bridges
- Journals as bridges to self
- Diaries as bridges to life
- Logs as bridges to data

Naturalist
- Nature's bridges to past
- Natural bridges such as vines
- Bridges in weather, climate & environment (jet stream, trade winds)
- Environmental bridges (conservation strategies)
- Natural bridges to future (evolution)

Figure 3.4

IRI/SkyLight Training and Publishing

The Process

Once the questions are fully developed, the problem solving begins. This process follows a fairly well-accepted and well-known method of gathering facts, analyzing the problem, generating alternatives, and advocating a solution or position. In this way, the problem-solving process evolves quite naturally. For example, in the investigation of the concept of bridges, students might choose to solve the problem of building model bridges that fit certain specifications, or they might explore the genetic bridges of DNA.

Thematic Learning

Gathering Facts

To gather information, of course, students engage in reading, interviewing, and searching for resources. They may work in small groups or individually. Either way, the materials they gather must help define the problem. How the data is gathered is determined by the ingenuity, talent, and persistence of the investigators. Once students select the problem area of focus—such as the physics of building model bridges or the genetic factors of DNA bridges to the past—they can make decisions about how to best proceed in the fact-gathering process.

Analyzing the Problem

Armed with the necessary facts, students must organize and analyze their notes and documents into various formats, including charts, drawings, models, writings, diagrams, and illustrations. In this phase of the investigation, the learner focuses on making sense of the available information by prioritizing the data and weight of certain aspects of the problem.

In fact, it is in this phase of analysis that a solution begins to emerge. Although the solution may change several times, the processing of the information starts the mind looking for patterns and possible solutions. For example, as students learn about the principles of stress as related to building different types of model bridges, they may have insight about adjustments to a design they are studying.

Generating Alternatives

Students can conduct brainstorming sessions to investigate alternative ideas. Such a session is useful in helping students resist the temptation to jump to conclusions about the best possible idea. It is important for the team or individual to stay open minded about all ideas. They must be willing to embrace any solution that offers the critical elements that satisfy the problem under consideration. More specifically, students working on the bridges theme may discover a number of solutions to obstacles that occur in building a viable model bridge.

Advocating a Solution or Position

As the investigation comes to a close, the investigators must use their best information to prepare their findings in an appropriate format. This is

Thematic Learning

the phase where the final work is done, when students creatively shape their findings into a presentable and persuasive format to advocate a solution or position. Students working on the bridge theme, for example, construct final prototypes, field test their models, or develop presentations on literary bridging. This will depend on what discipline areas they are using to investigate the concept of bridges.

At the end of the investigation, the students take their products, processes, or presentations to a public forum to communicate their original findings. The "publication" of their work gives closure to an investigation that has involved much of the team's time and effort. Celebrations are in order, also.

The Criteria

The thematic unit developed as an authentic investigation involves five critical criteria: relevancy, richness, relatedness, rigor, and recursiveness (Stanciak 1996; Doll 1993). The following rubric (fig. 3.5) illustrates possible criteria for each of these categories using the bridges theme.

Relevance

Learning that is relevant relates to students' lives. Knowledge for knowledge's sake may be desirable at some level of academic endeavor, but relevant learning speaks directly to students. For example, examining bridges in the community adds stimulation to the study of bridges in history, because the local bridges are real and known to the students. A field trip where students view and explore relevant bridges can be transferred into the abstract idea of bridges in one's life.

When a theme is relevant to students, as in the bridge example, students exhibit a natural interest and intrinsic motivation. In fact, when learning is relevant to students, they tend to focus and become task-oriented in their endeavors. They often work on their project on their own time, and may even get others involved by asking questions and telling stories about their work. At this point, the students take ownership of their learning because they sense how it impacts their lives.

Richness

Learning that is rich is not contrived to fit a theme. When there is richness in learning, there is no need to do soap sculptures of bridges in order to satisfy an artwork requirement. Instead, students developing prototypes of different kinds of bridges may decide to make soap sculptures in order to explore various bridge designs. Richness means that the unit of study presents problematic situations that allow for multidimensional learning. That is to say, students are led into activities that require authentic use of their many intelligences to learn about and work on current problems. These activities also allow them to express what they know or are learning.

Richness in theme-based problems involves moving from pencil/paper tasks to multidimensional learning, such as using simulations or building

Bridges Rubric

Integrated Curriculum

Theme/Thread: *Bridges: What Do They Connect?*

Criteria	Not Yet	On Our Way!	This Is It!
RELEVANCE (Real)	Inert knowledge *Bridges (types)*	Relates conceptually to one subject *Bridges in art/ architecture & design*	Real world application *Concept of bridges*
RICHNESS (Multidimensional)	Contrived fit *Pencil/paper tasks and tests about types of bridges*	Singular dimension *Design, sketch paint, draw bridges*	Breadth and depth across intelligences *A developed exhibition of models of bridges.*
RELATEDNESS (Connected)	No obvious connection across disciplines *Bridges of the world*	Superficial connections across disciplines *Bridges as structures*	Natural, genuine connections across disciplines *Bridges as concept in econ., lit., sci., dev., etc.*
RIGOR (Higher-Order Thinking)	Pour and store, recall and regurgitate *Name, locate & describe bridges*	Challenge: follow rigorous procedure *Bridges: making & breaking*	Struggle: getting stuck and getting unstuck *Bridges: Problem-solving what ifs...*
RECURSIVENESS (Transfer)	Singular opportunity for concept/ skill development *Bridges as architecture*	Multiple opportunities for concept/ skill development *Bridges across contexts (conjunctions, transitions)*	Transfer of skills and concepts to novel situations through problem solving *Personally relevant bridges*

Extrapolated from Stanciak 1996; Doll 1993

Figure 3.5

Thematic Learning

models. To provide a rich learning experience, teachers teach with breadth and depth across the multiple intelligences, instead of didactically. Rich learning experiences involve student immersion through inviting designs that hook students into authentic tasks.

Relatedness

Students combine several disciplines when investigating a theme. When these disciplines are connected authentically within an umbrella unit, they are related. Consider the bridge unit. Students may draw bridges in drafting class, develop literary bridges in language arts class, and study famous bridges in history class. However, true connectedness across the disciplines occurs when they are related through a project or performance. For example, relatedness between math and science is evident in the bridge unit when students build models of bridges that meet actual load specifications and style requirements.

Rigor

Rigor involves learning that is challenging and that dictates higher-order thinking operations such as problem solving, mindful decision making, and creative ideation. It does *not* involve "pouring and storing" information, where students focus on recall and regurgitation of information. Students must predict, infer, compare, prioritize, generalize, classify, categorize, hypothesize, analyze, and evaluate in a rigorous curriculum. In the bridges theme, students are expected to experience many of these higher-order thinking tasks to build a model, research DNA as a bridge to the past, or evaluate transitional paragraphs as bridges in literature.

When students are truly challenged, they experience the intended rigor of thematic learning. Students solve challenging problems through perseverance, ingenuity, and personal commitment. When they have solved a problem, they are able to feel a genuine, heartfelt sense of accomplishment. Learners know when they have met a challenge, and there is no way to counterfeit that experience. It is at this stage of struggle that students encounter the rigor of an authentic investigation.

Recursiveness

Recursiveness guarantees transfer of learning. It is the difference between a single opportunity for concept/skill development, which is domain specific, and the transfer of learning across disciplines and across contexts in life. Learning is enhanced when it can be decontextualized and applied to new situations.

Recursive themes are themes that are encountered over and over again in life as well as in school. Bridges can be used as such a theme. As illustrated throughout this discussion, the concept of bridges is easily "bridged" or transferred from bridges in poetry to bridges in families. In school, recursiveness is most likely to occur when the disciplines make concerted efforts to identify the big ideas and life skills that run through all content. These ideas appear at "teachable moments," and teachers can identify them and eventually use them in diverse contexts.

Thematic Learning

Who Are the Key Players and What Are Their Roles?

Teachers

In thematic learning, teachers are collaborators. Interdisciplinary teams are a basic staffing structure that is the foundation of thematic units. Although elementary teachers are responsible for most of the discipline areas, they can work with colleagues to plan units. Using this type of "think-tank" model, teachers can greatly enhance the units they teach in their classes.

At the middle school and high school level, teams of four to five teachers from different disciplines can work together. Teachers from different departments and fields of study can talk to one another in a formal forum and learn what is going on in the building. In this way, content becomes integrated as teachers communicate and discover themes that connect concepts, skills, and attitudes across disciplines.

David Johnson once said, "The more diverse the team, the richer the product" (Johnson and Johnson 1986). Teacher teams should be diverse not only in content and discipline, but also in gender, age, years of experience, personalities, learning styles, and expertise. Music, art, P.E., gifted, reading, and speech teachers; guidance counselors; resource people; and other staff that works with students should also be included in the teams. While these people may not be permanent members of every team, they can offer additional expertise as adjuncts to team planning sessions. In addition, they can provide an opportunity for further communication among staff about curricular content that ties into the school activities. Team adjuncts also create opportunities for further flexibility in scheduling and activities for the team as they actually begin to implement the unit.

Students

Students are active learners in thematic learning. As active learners, they conduct investigations that involve research, planning, evaluating, and production. Students work both together and in small groups. If students are to really understand what they are learning, they must interact with others during the learning process (Vygotsky 1978). Thus, the students' active/interactive role is essential for the thematic units of study to be considered authentic models of learning.

Why Do Themes Work?

Thematic Learning

Caine and Caine's research (1991) is perhaps the most succinct resource available on brain-compatible learning for deep understanding and long-term application. Their study synthesizes current brain research and presents it in a reader-friendly format. Based on the following principles, their work has grave implications for holistic learning embraced by thematic instruction.

1. The brain is a parallel processor, suggesting that good teaching orchestrates the learner's experience for "whole-brain learning."
2. Learning engages the entire physiology. It is as natural as breathing but can be nurtured or inhibited.
3. The search for meaning is innate. It occurs naturally and flourishes in a healthy, inviting environment.
4. The search for meaning occurs through patterning. Pattern-seeking devices of the mind use problem-solving and critical thinking to reorganize ideas and chunk them into patterns.
5. Emotions are critical to patterning. It is impossible to isolate the affective from the cognitive.
6. The brain processes parts and wholes simultaneously. Therefore, good teaching builds on skills over time, and, at the same time, embeds learning in relevant, holistic experiences.
7. Learning involves both focused attention and peripheral perception. It is shaped by things such as art, music, and tone of voice beyond the learner's focused attention.
8. Learning always involves conscious and unconscious processes, indicating that "active processing" is a necessary component of a quality learning experience.
9. We have at least two different types of memory: a spatial memory system and a set of systems for rote learning. This implies that teaching needs to facilitate both memorization and long-term transfer.
10. We understand and remember best when facts and skills are embedded in natural, spatial memory, inferring that real-life activity is conducive to deep understanding.
11. Learning is enhanced by challenge and inhibited by threat, suggesting the need for a state of "relaxed alertness" in students.
12. Each brain is unique, suggesting the need for multi-faceted teaching, with freedom of choices structured into the experiences.

Robert Sylwester (1996) also delineates findings that point toward holistic ideas, which make up the heart and soul of themes. He speaks of the uniqueness of each person's brain and the way it impacts how and when individuals learn. The nature of themes as a focused yet open-ended framework for diverse learning is a likely match to the myriad styles and needs of the learners.

When Can Themes Be Used Effectively?

ELEMENTARY EXAMPLE

It's a Seed of an Idea

✳ Brainstorm a Bank of Themes

Select an interest (plants) as a starting point for a brainstorm of related ideas. Then, select a working title for the theme. Here is a short brainstormed list of themes related to plants:

Living things
Growing things
Family trees
Seeds
Growth

✳ Pose Questions

Generate a long list of questions related to the theme. Try to get a focus on the theme. At the same time, broaden the theme idea if possible. Listed below are some sample questions:

What is a family?
What is a tree?
What is a family tree?
Does everyone have one?
Can you grow a family tree?
How do you grow a family tree?
Are families really trees?
What other kinds of trees are there?
What other kinds of tree families are there?
What tree has a family?
Can you hug a tree?
Can you hug a family tree?
Is growth like a tree?
Do trees have roots?
Do families have roots?

Revise the theme's working title so that it elaborates the ideas and gives focus to the thematic work. The theme title "Growing and the Family Tree: Where Are Your Roots?" is selected here to take the theme beyond the science unit on plants and living things. By using the idea of a "family tree" and "roots," the theme stretches beyond the science realm and into the social realm of family

**Thematic
Learning**

history, heritage, and family roots. This metaphorical "tree" adds rich possibilities for a comprehensive unit. It opens the theme to several related and fertile ideas.

The theme is now turned into a problem to solve. This problem, or challenge, invites investigation in many areas, as noted by the initial web of ideas (fig. 3.6) and the multiple intelligences grid of activities (fig. 3.7).

In turn, the steps of investigating an idea are followed: gathering information, analyzing the information, generating alternatives and advocating a solution or position.

✳ Turn the Theme into a Problem-Solving Investigation

Gather Facts

Use the webbing strategy to gather initial ideas about the theme activities and learning experiences. Explore the breadth of the theme to see if it stretches across various disciplines.

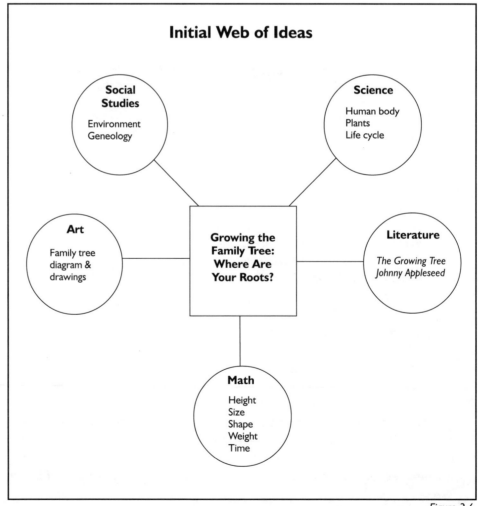

Figure 3.6

Analyze the Problem

Once the initial web is done, try to analyze the problem further by developing a grid of ideas based on the multiple intelligences (see fig. 3.7).

Thematic Learning

Generate Alternatives

The teacher and the students use the grid and the web to select alternative ideas to investigate. These investigations may vary from subject to subject. They may involve whole groups, small groups, or individual work. Inherent in the learning areas are problem-solving tasks and various learning opportunities. For instance, students might create a family pedigree of their DNA (genetic traits).

Advocate a Solution or Position

Students use presentations, portfolios, products, and performances to advocate a solution based on the various learnings in the thematic unit. For example, students might showcase their photo portfolios depicting their changes throughout the year. In addition, they might take their potted plants and replant them in the schoolyard.

In this phase, the theme is beginning to wind down. Prepare to conclude the unit.

Multiple Intelligences Grid of Activities
Growing & the Family Tree: Where Are the Roots?

Visual	Verbal	Logical	Musical	Bodily	Interpersonal	Intrapersonal	Naturalist
Slides or microscope	Reading diaries, journals from family	Graphing growth of self; plants; family	Music of various generations	Planting seedling	Interviewing parents	Geneology: family tree w/pictures	Growing beans
Pictures of growing things	Writing about "family roots"	Diagraming family tree	Growing plants to music	Nature walk	Interviewing grandparents	Journal of investigation	Growing grass
Family videos	Keeping a plant growth log	Surveys, statistics, data & information about plants, or families, etc.	Nature music (waves, wind, birds)	"Hug"-a-tree unit	Small group research projects	Diary of growth	Planting a garden
Photograph albums	Telling about family heritage	DNA—% of inherited traits, family pedigree	Music of various cultural heritages	Exploring attic, closets, cellars, for family heirlooms, etc.	Group murals of pond, rain forest, field, etc.	Log of learning about family	Tracing natural life cycle in pond
Sketching family members	Old newspapers, yearbooks, scrapbooks	Demographic information	Performing music of an era	Role-playing family heroes	Partner work on projects	Scrapbook	Hatching butterflies
Illustrations of plant parts, etc.	Listening to family stories; oral histories		Appreciating music of a region		Relating to others in family history	Portfolio	Raising tadpoles to frogs
Mapping a flower garden						Reflective quotes for sayings from family	"Adopting" a tree
Films of other generations							Studying rain forests for life cycles

Figure 3.7

IRI/SkyLight Training and Publishing

MIDDLE SCHOOL EXAMPLE
Rites of Passage: Rights or Responsibilities?

✳ Brainstorm a Bank of Ideas

Select an interest (rites and rights) as a starting point for a brainstorm of related ideas. Then, select a working title for the theme. Here is a short brainstormed list of themes related to rites and rights:

> Home alone
> Graduation
> Babysitting
> Driver's license
> First love
> Learning to read and write
> Personal style
> Rights of passage
> Adolescence
> Growing up
> Personal best

✳ Pose Questions

Using the theme you have chosen, generate a long list of related questions. Try to get a focus for the thematic unit. At the same time, broaden the theme idea if possible. Listed below are some sample questions:

> Whose rights?
> What passage?
> Path or pass?
> Righteous passage?
> Passing on the right?
> The right way to pass?
> Who cares?
> How do you do it?

Now, revise the working title to elaborate the idea(s) and give focus to the thematic work. In this example, the theme title. "Rites of Passage: Rights or Responsibilities?" is selected to take the theme beyond the concept of "rites of passage" (staying home alone, graduation, first babysitting job, getting a driver's license). By using the play on words of "rites" and "rights," the theme addresses the idea that along with increased rights and freedoms comes increased burden and responsibility. The enriched title of this theme gives it a universiality of focus and a wealth of possibilities for diverse learning experiences.

Thematic Learning

With the expanded idea of "Rites of Passage: Rights or Responsibilities?," the theme takes on a problematic focus. This "problem" or challenge invites investigation in many areas, as noted by the initial web of ideas (fig. 3.8) and the multiple intelligences grid of activities (fig. 3.9).

In turn, the steps to investigating an idea are followed: gathering information, analyzing the information, generating alternatives, and advocating a solution or position.

✳ Turn the Theme into a Problem-Solving Investigation
Gather Facts

Use the webbing strategy to gather initial ideas about the theme activities and learning experiences. Explore the breadth of the theme to see if it stretches across various disciplines.

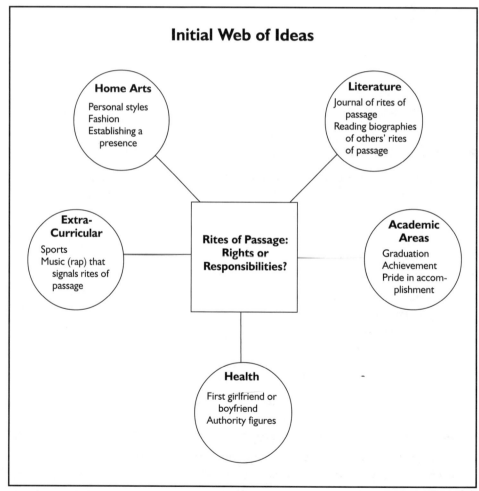

Figure 3.8

Analyze the Problem

Once the initial web is done, try to analyze further potential for the theme by developing a grid of ideas based on Gardner's multiple intelligences (fig. 3.9).

Thematic Learning

Generate Alternatives

The teacher and students use the grid and the web to select alternative ideas to investigate. These investigations may vary from subject to subject. They may involve whole groups, small groups, or individual work. Problem-solving tools and various learning opportunities are inherent in the learning areas.

For example, students may choose to role-play a formal rite of passage or develop their own home page on the Internet, which depicts their accomplishments.

Advocate a Solution or Position

Students use portfolios, products, performances, and presentations to report their many findings. For example, students might create a portfolio of their most significant achievements. Or, the class might present a play or video on rites of passage and rights and responsibilities that these passages represent.

In this phase, the unit is winding down to its conclusion. Prepare to conclude the unit.

Multiple Intelligences Grid of Activities
Rites of Passage: Rights or Responsibilities?

Visual	Verbal	Logical	Musical	Bodily	Interpersonal	Intrapersonal	Naturalist
Visualization of goals	Literature about rites of passage	Home page	Rap music that depicts rites of passage	Driver's license	Small group roles & responsibilities	Journaling	Babysitting (creating an environment)
Drawings	Stories about responsibility	Graphs & surveys of rites of passage data	Cultural music for rites of passage	Learning dances	Searching Internet for other cultures	Graduation (achievement; pride)	First overnight (adjusting to different environment)
Art log	Writing about multicultural rites of passage	Researching other cultures	Songs about work, duties, responsibility ("Nine to Five")	Advanced physical fitness feats	Relationships (first girl- or boyfriend)	Goals	Primative rites of passage in less-settled areas (in the bush of Australia, etc.)
Sketches	Writing poetry about rites of passage	Setting goals & strategic plans to achieve them	Composing lyrics about rites of passage	Learning to swim, ski, skate, etc.	Acceptance	Log of accomplishments	Health Issues (wellness, maturity, & fitness & adolescence)
Photographs	Expository pieces about pros & cons of rites of passage	Organizing data gathered	Appreciating music or various ages & stages of life	Experience with rights, responsibilities & rites of passage	Friends (Peer pressure or peer support)	Personal style, fashion, handwriting	
Video journal		Achievement in higher level math (algebra, trigonometry, calculus)				Own home page	
Films of significance						Reflective dialogues	
Using graphics to represent "rites" & "rights"							

Figure 3.9

IRI/SkyLight Training and Publishing

HIGH SCHOOL EXAMPLE
Do You Mind My Habits of Mind?

**Thematic
Learning**

✳ Brainstorm a Bank of Ideas

Use the area of interest (habits or habits of mind) as a starting point for a brainstorm of related ideas. Then, select a working title for the theme development. Following is a list of brainstormed theme ideas:

Habits
Behaviors
States of mind
Mind matters
Do minds matter?
Matters of the mind
Intelligent behaviors
Dispositions
Attitudes
Mind over matter

✳ Pose Questions

Using the theme choice, generate a long list of related questions. Try to get a focus for the thematic unit. At the same time, broaden the theme idea if possible.

What are habits?
What are habits of mind?
Can I change my habits of mind?
How do I develop habits of mind?
Are habits of mind good?
Do you mind your habits?
Do your habits mind?
Do you mind?
Who cares?
Who knows?
How do you know?
What evidence is there?
Do you mind your habits of mind?

Now, revise the working title to elaborate the ideas and give focus to the thematic work. In this illustration, the theme title "Do You Mind My Habits of Mind?" is chosen for the intriguing question it sets up. The question implies that habits of mind can be good and bad. For example, habits of mind that benefit the individual are perseverance, craftsmanship, and tolerance. Habits of mind that

Thematic Learning

probably do not benefit the mind are sloppiness, impulsivity, and bias. By using the question "Do You Mind My Habits of Mind?," the theme is opened up in a playful, yet profound way. Once students are aware of their habits of mind, metacognitively or reflectively, they are able to control them. The possibilities of this theme idea are invigorating as well as endless!

With the expanded idea of "Do You Mind My Habits of Mind?," the theme takes on a problematic focus. This problem, or challenge, invites investigation in many areas, as noted by the initial web of ideas (fig. 3.10) and the multiple intelligences grid of activities (fig. 3.11).

In turn, the steps to investigating an idea are followed: gathering information, analyzing the information, generating alternatives, and advocating a solution or position.

✳ Turn the Theme into a Problem-Solving Investigation

Gather Facts

Use the web strategy to gather initial ideas about the themes. This web uses traditional subject matter of the theme to validate that the theme reaches across different content areas.

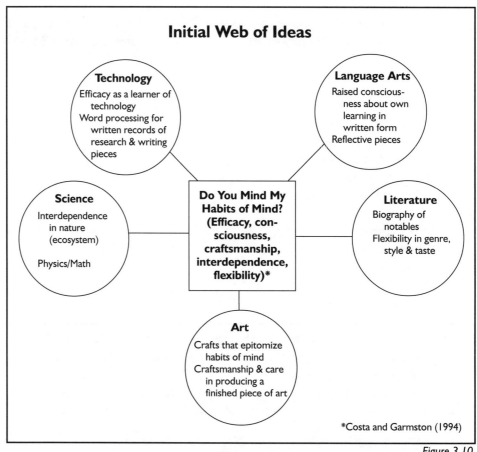

Initial Web of Ideas

Technology
Efficacy as a learner of technology
Word processing for written records of research & writing pieces

Language Arts
Raised consciousness about own learning in written form
Reflective pieces

Science
Interdependence in nature (ecosystem)
Physics/Math

Do You Mind My Habits of Mind? (Efficacy, consciousness, craftsmanship, interdependence, flexibility)*

Literature
Biography of notables
Flexibility in genre, style & taste

Art
Crafts that epitomize habits of mind
Craftsmanship & care in producing a finished piece of art

*Costa and Garmston (1994)

Figure 3.10

Analyze the Problem

Once the initial web is completed, develop a grid of ideas to analyze further potential for the theme (fig. 3.11). These activities are categorized according to Gardner's multiple intelligences to show how well the theme encompasses learning in various ways.

Generate Alternatives

The teacher and students use the grid and the web to select alternative ideas to investigate. These investigations may vary from subject to subject. They may include whole group, small group, or individual work. Problem-solving tools and various learning opportunities are inherent in the learning areas. For instance, some may want to pursue changing a habit of theirs, while others may want to analyze the habits of mind of a key character in a novel or in history.

Advocate a Solution or Position

Students use portfolios, products, performances, and presentations to report the many findings they have pursued during the thematic unit. Prepare to bring closure to the theme. For example, students may submit a journal of reflections on their habits of mind or small groups might present a role-play of desirable and undesirable habits of mind.

Thematic Learning

Multiple Intelligences Grid of Activities
Do You Mind My Habits of Mind

Visual	Verbal	Logical	Musical	Bodily	Interpersonal	Intrapersonal	Naturalist
Drawing	Poetry of people	Survey companies for habits of mind valued in careers	Craftsmanship in performance	Crafts	Dialogue w/family on your habits of mind	Regime for getting up	Evidence of habits of mind in nature's beasts
Sketching	Character analysis in literature	Trace development of habits of mind	Learning craft of playing instrument	Physical habits	Agree/disagree with friends on habits of mind	Journal of daily routine	Interdependence of ecosystem
Model building	News article	Craftmanship and accuracy in competition & calculation	Appreciating craft of jazz, blues, country, classical, etc.	Routines for exercising, etc.	Shadow someone who displays habits of mind you admire	Notes of habits of mind (evidence)	Rainforest (ecological habits)
Photography as craft of skill & vision	Biography of others' habits of mind	Computer craftsmanship	Create map of habits of mind	Change of habit (smoking, biting nails, twisting hair)	Promote tolerance & flexibility in multicultural world	Developing raised consciousness through reflection & meditation	Life cycle (save the earth)
Visualizing crafted product	Reading personal interest stories in newsgroups	Efficacy of student to think logically, solve problems, use math to make sense of world					
Demonstrating flexibility in changing, revising, shifting focus of art	Flexible in revision & editing of writing						

Figure 3.11

Where Is More Information?

**Thematic
Learning**

Art, Mind, and Brain by H. Gardner

Circles of Learning: Cooperation in the Classroom by R. Johnson and D. Johnson

Cognitive Coaching: A Foundation for Renaissance Schools by A. L. Costa and R. J. Garmston

Connecting Curriculum through Interdisciplinary Instruction by J. H. Loundsbury

Curriculum Guide for the Education of Gifted High School Students by J. Currey and J. Samara

Explosion of Neurons by R. Sylwester

Frames of Mind: The Theory of Multiple Intelligences by H. Gardner

Holistic Learning: A Teacher's Guide to Integrated Studies by J. Miller Jr., B. Cassie, and S. Drake

If the Shoe Fits: How to Develop Multiple Intelligences in the Classroom by C. Chapman

Inside the Brain: Revolutionary Discoveries of How the Mind Works by R. Kotulak

Integrating Curricula with Multiple Intelligences: Teams, Themes, and Threads by R. Fogarty and J. Stoehr

Integrating Mathematics across the Curriculum by H. Martin

Integrating the Curricula: A Collection edited by R. Fogarty

Interdisciplinary Curriculum: Design and Implementation by H. H. Jacobs

ITI: The Model: Integrated Thematic Instruction by S. Kovalik

Making Connections: Teaching and the Human Brain by R. N. Caine and G. Caine

The Mindful School: How to Integrate the Curricula by R. Fogarty

Multiple Intelligences Centers and Projects by C. Chapman and L. Freeman

Multiple Intelligences in the Mathematics Classroom by H. Martin

Multiple Intelligences: The Theory in Practice by H. Gardner

The Newsletter of the Interdisciplinary Curriculum and Instruction Network by L. A. Stanciak

Smart Schools: From Training Memories to Educating Minds by D. N. Perkins

The Team Process: A Handbook for Teachers by E. Y. Merenbloom

Thinking Frames by D. N. Perkins

To Open Minds by H. Gardner

What's My Thinking Now?

Reflections:

....
....
....
....
....
....
....

Comments:

....
....
....
....
....
....
....

Questions:

....
....
....
....
....
....
....

IRI/SkyLight Training and Publishing

How Can I Use Themes?

Use this outline to apply themes to your content and classroom.

✳ **Brainstorm a bank of themes**

....
....
....
....
....
....
....
....
....
....
....
....
....
....

✳ **Pose questions**

....
....
....
....
....
....
....
....
....
....
....
....
....
....

How Can I Use Themes?

✳ **Turn the theme into an investigation**

Gather Facts (Web)

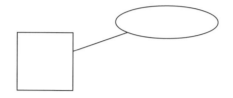

Analyze the Problem (Grid)

V/S	V/L	M/L	M/R	B/K	Inter.	Intra.	Nat.

Generate Alternatives (Problem Solving)

....
....
....
....
....
....

Advocate a Solution or Position (Performance)

....
....
....
....
....
....

PROJECT LEARNING

Inventing is a combination of brains and materials.
The more brains you use, the less materials you need.

—Charles F. Kettering

Project Learning

What Is Project Learning?

Project learning is authentic learning. It involves tangible, visible, and personally tailored projects for students. In addition, project learning provides inviting and productive learning experiences. Science projects that require knowledge, talent, and creative endeavors from students and sometimes their family members, neighbors, and friends exemplify the authentic learning of hands-on, trial-and-error project learning experiences. The nature of the project is dynamic as it goes through conception, configuration, contradiction, confusion, reconfiguration, and eventually culmination and celebration. This is hands-on learning in all its glory. It's learning with a known focus, expectations of productivity, and measurable results.

Project learning is organized around the creation, execution, and finished production of something. The project usually occurs within a reasonable time frame, ranging from a week to a semester, depending on the nature of the project. In addition, it often has well-defined parameters and published guidelines, such as a list of required materials, specifications in terms of performance, and definite timelines that must be adhered to. For example, book reports, research papers, multimedia presentations, and mechanical inventions are all projects that are strong organizers for tailoring the curriculum to students' interests, talents, and resourcefulness. Project learning encourages industry, collaboration, creativity, and integrated and experiential learning that forces closure with the submittal of a final product.

While project learning is sometimes considered to include presentations and performances—such as dramatic plays, musical productions, mock trials, and fashion shows—here it is confined to learning experiences that require a finished product that is object-related. The above-mentioned presentations and performances are included in the chapter on performance learning.

What Does Project Learning Look and Sound Like?

One might think that just as "a rose is a rose is a rose," "a project is a project is a project." Not true. Projects can be wide ranging and rich. Outlined in this section are the five kinds of projects that are possible as a curricular framework: structured projects, topic-related projects, genre-related projects, open-ended projects, and template projects.

Project Learning

Structured Projects

Structured projects have specific limitations. Certain criteria are predetermined, which usually include product specifications in terms of size, materials, and functions. Structured projects also tend to fall into a typical time frame, such as a semester, a quarter, or even a week. Examples of structured projects are the Egg Drop or the Catapult. The Egg Drop project requires students to construct a container that will protect an egg from breaking when dropped six feet. With the catapult project, students must construct a catapult that projects an object the length of a gymnasium. These projects have strict requirements that must be adhered to in terms of weight, distance, time, strength, or quality. If the product doesn't meet the specifications, it's back to the drawing board or the product is disqualified.

Topic-Related Projects

Topic-related projects evolve from a unit of study and often incorporate individual or small group assignments. Students choose a topic of interest from a list of options provided by the teacher or brainstormed by the students. These are typical, traditional kinds of school-related projects.

When a student chooses a topic that interests her, she is motivated to delve into it and produce a product that not only shows what she has learned, but also what personal significance it has for her. For example, a student studying World War II might select a topic from a list that ranges from specific people and places to concepts and events. Respectively, these topics might include Franco, Patton, and Mussolini; Philippines, Hiroshima, and Pearl Harbor; propaganda, persecution, and rationing; Battle of the Bulge, London Blitz, and Bataan Death March.

If the student chooses to study Patton, her completed project may be a multimedia presentation of the controversial general. If she decides to study the propaganda of World War II, her completed project may be a student magazine that features exposés on contemporary propaganda techniques.

Genre-Related Projects

Genre-related projects follow a particular genre, such as board games, in which the parameters are clear and the critical elements are present. The parameters of a genre-related project are somewhat set, although students have "creative license," unlike with the structured project. A genre-related

**Project
Learning**

project requires a student to honor the accepted tools of the trade and follow the "industry" guidelines.

Examples of genre-related projects include a biography of a puppet, a how-to speech, a children's storybook, a multimedia presentation, or an annual ice sculpture contest. In each of these examples, the project is related to a genre study that repeats each year. For instance, the teacher may include a biography unit in literature each year. In this unit, students read about creative geniuses. They also construct puppets of the character and present them in a puppet show.

Biography, children's literature, or speech are certainly governed by the qualities of their respective genres and students are expected to note these in their approach to their projects. However, there is plenty of room for creativity and novelty in the final projects that emerge.

Open-Ended Projects

Open-ended projects give minimal guidelines, few criteria, and little structure to encourage risk taking and innovative thinking. Open-ended projects promote discovery, insight, and invention. Students seek new ideas in open-ended projects and often find themselves in uncharted waters, which allows them to find unique solutions.

An open-ended project may take the form of a challenge, which provides a forum for thoughtful, relevant uses of students' ideas and skills. For example, undergraduate students in an industrial design class were challenged by General Electric to find a use for a plastic product called Lexon. The project had very few guidelines other than due dates and entry rules. The finished projects ranged from plastic cover plates for subdued stadium exit lighting to a reflector for life-saving devices.

Other examples include designing a piece of furniture or a kitchen utensil for the geriatric population; building a car powered through light-sensitivity and solar energy; and constructing a kite for a radio station promotion. Each of these projects is purposely open ended to encourage creativity and risk taking, yet each has a functional side valued in a traditional way.

Template Projects

Projects framed around a preexisting template naturally have predetermined material, but they also have tailor-made material. For example, a school newspaper has a generally accepted structure; therefore, creating a template is a good idea. Although the structure is the same, students are free to be as creative and clever as possible within the given framework.

Another example is a school yearbook. While the template varies little, the creative conceptualizations of the team become obvious as the project evolves. Because each yearbook has its own written and artistic themes and photos, the mark of its creators is indelible.

How Does Project Learning Work?

In the three-story intellect process, as depicted by Holmes' words in, the learner researches to gather ideas, processes ideas by developing a prototype, and applies ideas by creating a completed project. The steps include electing, selecting, researching, reading, gathering facts, sketching, drawing, illustrating, developing prototypes, trying, testing, evaluating, revising, revamping, reconceptualizing, trying again, testing, and evaluating.

Project Learning

Three-Story Intellect Model for Project Development

There are one-story intellects,

two-story intellects,

three-story intellects with skylights.

All fact-collectors,

who have no aim beyond their facts,

are one-story men.

Two-story men compare, reason, generalize,

using the labor of fact collectors as their own.

Three-story men idealize, imagine, predict;

their best illumination comes from above, through the skylight.

—Oliver Wendell Holmes

While Holmes may not have intended the three stories to be sequential, they do provide a viable mental model when envisioned as the scaffolding needed to construct authentic projects in the classroom. In the first level of activities, information and other materials are gathered. During the second phase, students begin to form ideas from the information. At the third stage, the project is completed and evaluated.

In fig. 4.1, appropriate learning strategies are delineated within each of the three stories to illustrate how naturally and easily the multiple intelligences are incorporated and integrated into the learning.

✳ First-Story Intellect: Gathering Activities

A project is either selected by students from a bank of ideas or, in the case of the structured project, by the teacher. After the guidelines are set by the teacher, the initial stages of reading, researching, interviewing, and fact gathering consume the student or student team. This phase of the project engages students in tasks they are most familiar with in the school setting: using references, finding resources, and collecting data. During this initial

The Three-Story Intellect with Multiple Intelligences

3 APPLYING
Try and Test

Verbal: using metaphors, similes, analogies, puns, plays on words

Visual: visualizing, imagining, dreaming, envisioning, symbolizing

Logical: evaluating, judging, refining, creating analogies, reasoning, critiquing

Musical: composing, improvising, critiquing, performing, conducting

Bodily: constructing, dramatizing, peforming, experimenting, sculpting

Interpersonal: debating, compromising, mediating, arbitrating,

Intrapersonal: meditating, intuiting, innovating, inventing, creating

Naturalist: forecasting, predicting, interrelating, synthesizing, categorizing

PROCESSING 2 Crystallize Ideas

Verbal: paraphrasing, essay writing, labeling, reporting, organizing

Visual: sketching, mapping, diagramming, illustrating, cartooning

Logical: graphing, comparing, classifying, ranking, analyzing, coding

Musical: playing, selecting, singing, responding to music

Bodily: rehearsing, studying, experimenting, investigating

Interpersonal: expressing, telling/retelling, arguing, discussing

Intrapersonal: studying, self-assessing, interpreting, processing

Naturalist: categorizing, sorting, relating, classifying

GATHERING 1 Research Project

Verbal: questioning, reading, listing, telling, writing, finding, listening, documenting

Visual: viewing, observing, seeing, describing, showing

Logical: recording, collecting, logging, documenting

Musical: listening, gathering, audiotaping, attending concerts

Bodily: preparing, exploring, investigating, interviewing

Interpersonal: interacting, teaming, interviewing, affirming

Intrapersonal: reflecting, expressing, reacting, journaling

Naturalist: observing, catching, identifying, photographing

Figure 4.1

phase, the groundwork is laid for the inventiveness of the later two stages. Having necessary and accurate information creates a sound base for a project. Therefore, if the early parts of the project are done with care and integrity, the project is likely to progress smoothly.

In addition to the strategies depicted in figure 4.1, myriad activities appropriate for this first phase encompass nitty-gritty pieces such as those listed below.

Project Learning

Gathering Ideas: Researching the Project

Reading for background information

Researching and taking notes

Building a reference list

Interviewing experts

Viewing films and videos

Developing an outline

Talking with peers

Surfing the Internet

Checking and double-checking sources

Visiting sites

Gathering charts, maps, illustrations

Once the project begins to take shape, students move effortlessly to the next level of the intellect. The nature of their activities shifts from gathering information to analyzing it.

✳ Second-Story Intellect: Processing Activities

As a project enters the second-story intellect, students become immersed in facts and begin to try to make sense of them. They discover that some information is relevant and some is not. At this level, the mind tries to (1) analyze whatever information it has, (2) sort the information into meaningful chunks, and (3) synthesize it in order to move the project forward. Of course, if the project is a team effort, the group members must find ways to share their information.

**Project
Learning**

Following are activities often employed at this level.

Processing Information: Crystallizing Ideas

Brainstorming ideas	Reconciling conflicting data
Analyzing data	Finding a focus
Charting information	Assigning a theme
Drawing and sketching models	Creating a metaphor
Drafting ideas	Looking for patterns
Developing prototypes	Seeking connections
Filling in missing information	Playing with ideas
Visualizing the big picture	Finding materials

The timeline of the project may begin to stretch at this phase because it is not clear what the project's focus is, or because of obstacles such as unavailable or wrong materials, incomplete research, or unproductive team members. This is the time when it may be necessary to facilitate the project in order to keep it on track. However, it is not a disaster if the project gets off track. Sometimes this forces students to revisit the project from a new perspective. In any case, as anyone who has embarked on an extensive project will attest to, it is this "messing around" stage, or processing, that is absolutely crucial to the quality, originality, and effectiveness of the final product.

It is important to note that even though the three-story intellect model implies that one level builds on the one before it, the true nature of any project suggests that a lot of back-and-forth activity occurs. Students return to the gathering stages many times throughout the second level activities, and they are certain to engage in third-level activities as well.

✳ Third-Story Intellect: Applying Activities

At this point in the project, the students understand what needs to be done to complete it. They divide and prioritize tasks, check timelines, take any necessary emergency measures, and stay alert. When the project reaches final form, it is reviewed, tested, revised, and repaired.

Following are activities in the third-story intellect.

Applying Ideas: Trying and Testing

Model building	Evaluative testing
Construction	Peer review
Assembling	Self-assessment
Synthesizing ideas	Evaluation against criteria
Rethinking or reconceptualizing	Expert review
Finishing touches	Final submittals
Decorative details	Celebrations

Project Learning

Of course, Holmes' three-story intellect is simply a framework applied to the process of developing a project. Yet, the three stories do trace the process quite naturally. Each project passes through the similar stages of development: (1) an attempt at finding a focal point; (2) a first draft and skeletal models; and (3) a finished product. This three-step process is important in the project learning design.

Who Are the Key Players and What Are Their Roles?

Teachers

Teachers may take a directive role in some projects and a non-authoritative role in others. For example, structured projects require a teacher to be directive because the parameters of the project are strictly set. On the other hand, open-ended projects require a teacher to act as a coach or mentor. What role the teacher takes depends not only on the project type, but also on the age of the students, the sophistication of the project, the timelines, and the style of the teacher.

Students

Students take the role of active, hands-on learners. They are responsible for the final product. Many projects in project learning require students to work together in teams, with each person responsible for certain tasks.

**Project
Learning**

Why Does Project Learning Work?

The research base for project learning extends to the field of inquiry learning. Inquiry learning leads students to investigate why things work or why phenomena occur. In the science classroom, inquiry learning is referred to as hands-on science, inductive learning, or concept formation.

The rationale that supports the kind of inductive learning that is inherent in authentic project work is related to its developmental nature. Based on the research of Piaget (1952), learners move through various levels of understanding, starting with the concrete and moving through the representational and abstract. For example, young learners first use concrete math manipulations, then pictorial representations of objects. Eventually, they use abstract symbols to understand numbers. Similarly, novices use all three developmental levels to assimilate and accommodate conceptual understandings.

Another example is learning to classify by sorting rocks (concrete); grouping pictures of leaves (symbolic); and reading about classifying species by their critical attributes (abstract). The understanding flows from a developmental model of learning.

By learning through concrete, symbolic, and abstract ways, students engage in developmental stages of learning (Piaget 1952; Vygotsky 1978; Bruner 1973; Taba in Joyce and Weil 1980). By working with an authentic project, students begin to grasp concepts while putting their ideas on paper and eventually into a working prototype. In this way, abstract ideas are anchored for long-term memory and learning is ingrained in the mind of the learner.

When Can Project Learning Be Used Effectively?

ELEMENTARY EXAMPLE
Biography: Puppet and Presentation

Project Learning

✳ Type of Project

Genre-related

✳ Learning Context

This project exposes students to creative geniuses across many fields of endeavor—the arts, music, literature, athletics, dance, science, history, and technology. The students select and read a biography and produce a puppet show based on the person studied. In this example, the three-story intellect model is illustrated using the life of Leonardo da Vinci.

✳ First-Story Intellect: Gathering Activities

Read

The World of Leonardo, Time-Life Library of Art, or another biography of choice.

Research

da Vinci's scientific inventions (the life preserver, propellers, helicopter, mechanical car, and the spinning wheel); art and architecture (studies of the human body, nature themes, the *Mona Lisa,* animals, perspective, and motion); personal traits, characteristics, and life story (left-handedness, journals and sketch books, move from Florence to Milan, sculptures and paintings, style, etc.).

Interview

Interview someone who has traveled to Italy and seen da Vinci's work.

View

Look at books, slides, and videos of da Vinci's art.

Listen

Listen to audiotapes about the artist.

Visit

Go to a museum to see and learn about his art and life.

**Project
Learning**

Search the Internet

Use the Internet's search engines to learn about da Vinci, and/or set up an interview with an expert online.

✳ Second-Story Intellect: Processing Activities

Sketch

Try to sketch da Vinci from his famous self-portrait rendering.

Draw

Draw one of da Vinci's inventions or a figure from his paintings.

Calculate

Determine the following: how long da Vinci lived (1452–1519); how many paintings, sculptures, and inventions he produced; his most productive years; his annual or lifetime earnings; the number of sketch books he kept.

Generate

Gather quotations from da Vinci's journal. Generate a concept map of his biographic information. Create a first draft of a puppet show script.

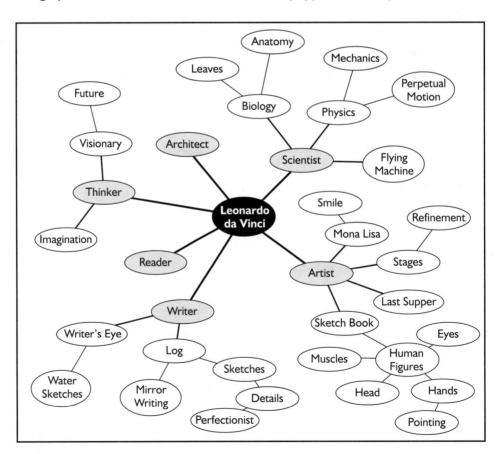

Develop a Prototype

Make a rough model in clay of a puppet face of da Vinci. Make the puppet with papier-mâché. Experiment with material and cloth for the puppet. Plan the scene.

**Project
Learning**

✴ Third-Story Intellect: Applying Activities

Try

Do a trial run with the puppet and try out the movements.

Test

Test the speech that the da Vinci puppet will make by reading the first draft script.

Evaluate

Rehearse in front of someone.

Revise

Incorporate the feedback into a next draft of the puppet speech and continue to streamline the entire production.

Repeat Cycle

Rehearse, evaluate, incorporate feedback, fix things as necessary, and get ready for the real performance of the puppet show.

Showcase

Perform the puppet show and present the biographical figure to the audience using speeches, quotations, and props.

**Project
Learning**

MIDDLE SCHOOL EXAMPLE
The Many Ways of Knowing Our Community

✳ Type

Brochure Template

✳ Learning Context

In order to introduce parents to the concept of Howard Gardner's multiple intelligences, middle-schoolers develop a brochure. The brochure is complete with text, graphics design, formatting, and color. The content focuses on where in the community or surrounding areas families can experience the multiple intelligences. Once completed, the brochure is given to parents as a guide for summer, holiday, and weekend activities.

✳ First-Story Intellect: Gathering Activities

Read

Seven Kinds of Smart by Thomas Armstrong; articles and essays by Howard Gardner or *Frames of Mind* by Howard Gardner; *If the Shoe Fits: How to Develop Multiple Intelligences in the Classroom* by Carolyn Chapman; *Multiple Intelligences: A Collection* by Robin Fogarty and James Bellanca.

Research

Survey your class and other classes in the school to find out what they have used in the community and surrounding area for family field trips and other activities. Gather these ideas as they fit into the eight categories of the intelligences: visual/spatial, verbal/linguistic, mathematical/logical, musical/rhythmic, bodily/kinesthetic, interpersonal/social, intrapersonal/introspective, naturalist/physical world.

Interview

Talk with teachers, local officials, the Chamber of Commerce, local Realtors, merchants, and convention center personnel to collect more ideas about places of interest for students.

View

Look at promotional films, videos, brochures, and pamphlets to find out about specific events and locations.

Listen

Tune in to various radio and television stations to gather ideas from their broadcasts and promotions.

IRI/SkyLight Training and Publishing

Visit

Arrange to visit various sites to be included in the brochure in small groups with parent volunteers.

Search the Internet

Check the Internet for information on the multiple intelligences and places to go and things to see in and around the area.

Project Learning

✳ Second-Story Intellect: Processing Activities

Sketch

Sketch a layout of the brochure. Include a brief introduction to the intelligences and list the places and events that fit each.

Draw

Develop icons for each of the eight intelligences: verbal/linguistic, logical/mathematical, visual/spatial, musical/rhythmic, bodily/kinesthetic, interpersonal/social, intrapersonal/introspective, naturalist/physical world.

Calculate

Calculate the space needed for each category of intelligences; which categories will be biggest, smallest, and average size? Determine the total number of brochures to print. Estimate how much the brochure will cost in production time, printing costs, etc. Forecast how long the brochure will be current and accurate (i.e., the life of the brochure).

Generate

Generate ideas for the brochure cover and other artwork. Brainstorm type styles, layouts, writing styles, appropriate quotations, etc.

Develop a Prototype

Develop at least three prototypes of the multiple intelligences brochure for review.

✳ Third-Story Intellect: Applying Activities

Try

Let the class, the teachers, and or community officials look at the prototypes and give feedback.

Test

Test the favorite(s) of everyone in the class or other classes.

**Project
Learning**

Evaluate

Evaluate all data on the content and design and make decisions.

Revise

Revise the brochure as it takes shape.

Repeat the Cycle

Get feedback and revise the brochure accordingly. Complete the final product.

Showcase

Send the printed brochures home with every student in the school. Through a presentation, introduce students in the school to the multiple intelligences. Explain the idea of exercising the intelligences through the community.

HIGH SCHOOL EXAMPLE
Cataboom

**Project
Learning**

✳ **Type**

Structured Project

✳ **Learning Context**

Students research the historical significance and scientific background of the catapult by conducting interviews, visiting museums, and watching films. They use their knowledge of thrust, gravitational forces, and laws of motion to actually construct a catapult. Once it is constructed and tested under different conditions, the students demonstrate its use to others.

✳ **First-Story Intellect: Gathering Activities**

Read

Read about gravity, gravitational forces, thrust, laws of motion, simple machines.

Research

Research the use of catapults in ancient warfare. Discuss the javelin thrower in the Olympics. Find pictures/illustrations of catapults in history, in comics, etc.

Interview

Interview a science teacher and/or others about the laws of gravity and motion.

View

Watch *Braveheart* on video. Observe the use of ancient weapons in the film, including the catapult. View other films of similar genre.

Listen

Listen to the story of "David and Goliath" on tape. Compare a slingshot to a catapult.

Visit

Visit a museum with scientific inventions that use gravitational forces, thrust, etc.

Search the Internet

Seek information on the Internet about historical significance of catapults and other ancient warfare.

Project Learning

✳ Second-Story Intellect: Processing Activities

Sketch

Experiment with two or three sketches of a catapult for construction.

Draw

Draw the flow of the gravitational forces, laws of motion, and thrust. Label the illustrations.

Calculate

Calculate the load, thrust, and distance of a sack of flour, container of salt, pillow, bag of rice, bag of hard rolls, etc. Be ready to explain calculations.

Generate

Generate ideas for increasing the thrust of a catapult. List items to test with the catapult. Gather materials for constructing the catapult.

Develop a Prototype

Develop a scale model or prototype of the catapult. Specify the materials needed.

✳ Third-Story Intellect: Applying Activities

Try

Try building the catapult.

Test

Test various materials for improving construction. Use a number of different loads: sugar, sand, salt, rice, a pillow. Test different techniques.

Evaluate

Evaluate the results from the trials of the testing stage. Select the best materials, load, and thrust techniques.

Revise

Revise according to the evaluation results. Refine the catapult as necessary to improve the construction design.

Repeat the Cycle

Repeat the test, evaluate, and revise phases as needed for a final product.

Showcase

Demonstrate the finished catapult to others by using a variety of loads, etc.

IRI/SkyLight Training and Publishing

**Project
Learning**

Where Is More Information?

Best Practices for the Learner-Centered Classroom by R. Fogarty

Beyond I.Q.: A Triarchic Theory of Human Intelligences by R. J. Sternberg

Catch Them Thinking: A Handbook of Classroom Strategies by R. Fogarty and J. Bellanca

Catch Them Thinking in Science: A Handbook of Classroom Strategies by S. Berman

Classroom 2061: Activity-Based Assessments in Science Integrated with Mathematics and Language Arts by E. Hammerman and D. Musial

Cooperative Learning by S. Kagan

Flow: The Psychology of Optimal Experience by M. Csikszentmihalyi

Horace's School: Redesigning the American High School by T. Sizer

If Minds Matter: A Foreword to the Future (Vol. 1 & 2) by A. Costa, J. Bellanca, and R. Fogarty

If the Shoe Fits . . . : How to Develop Multiple Intelligences in the Classroom by C. Chapman

Metaphors of Mind: Conceptions of the Nature of Intelligence by R. J. Sternberg

The Mindful School: How to Teach for Transfer by R. Fogarty, D. Perkins, and J. Barell

Mind in Society: The Development of Higher Psychological Processes by L. S. Vygotsky

Models of Teaching by B. Joyce and M. Weil

Multiple Intelligences: A Collection by R. Fogarty and J. Bellanca

Multiple Intelligences Centers and Projects by C. Chapman and L. Freeman

The Multiple Intelligences Handbook by B. Campbell

Multiple Intelligences: The Theory in Practice by H. Gardner

Nature's Gambit: Child Prodigies and the Development of Human Potential by D. H. Feldman

The Origins of Intelligence in Children by J. Piaget

Patterns for Thinking: Patterns for Transfer by R. Fogarty and J. Bellanca

The School As a Home for the Mind by A. L. Costa

Seven Kinds of Smart: Identifying and Developing Your Many Intelligences by T. Armstrong

Six Thinking Hats by E. de Bono

Strategic Teaching and Learning: Cognitive Instruction in the Content Areas by B. F. Jones, A. Palincsar, D. S. Ogle, and E. G. Carr

Teaching and Learning through Multiple Intelligences by L. Campbell

What's My Thinking Now?

Reflections:

....
....
....
....
....
....
....

Comments:

....
....
....
....
....
....
....

Questions:

....
....
....
....
....
....
....

IRI/SkyLight Training and Publishing

How Can I Use Project Learning?

Use this outline to apply project learning to your content and classroom.

* **Type**

　..
　..

* **Learning Context**

　..
　..

* **First-Story Intellect: Gathering Activities**

Read

　..
　..
　..
　..

Research

　..
　..
　..
　..

Interview

　..
　..
　..
　..

View

　..
　..
　..
　..

How Can I Use Project Learning?

Listen

....
....
....
....
....

Visit

....
....
....
....
....

Search Internet

....
....
....
....
....

✳ Second-Story Intellect: Processing Activities

Sketch

....
....
....
....

Draw

....
....
....
....

How Can I Use Project Learning?

Calculate

....
....
....
....
....

Generate

....
....
....
....
....

Develop a Prototype

....
....
....
....
....

✳ Third-Story Intellect: Applying Activities

Try

....
....
....
....
....

How Can I Use Project Learning?

Test

....
....
....
....
....

Evaluate

....
....
....
....
....

Revise

....
....
....
....
....

Repeat the Cycle

....
....
....
....
....

Showcase

....
....
....
....
....

IRI/SkyLight Training and Publishing

SERVICE LEARNING

No one is useless in this world
who lightens the burden of another.
—Charles Dickens

Service Learning

What Is Service Learning?

The idea of learning in the context of serving others stems from experiential education. Immersion in the experience is the crux of service learning projects, which can extend into semester or yearly courses of study. Schools often partner with community leaders and agencies for civic-oriented projects. For example, students may help out at an old folks home or at a homeless shelter. In both cases, the students become a service arm of the agency or business.

The focus of service learning is twofold: (1) service to others, and (2) linking the service learning project to goals in the existing curriculum. Service programs become the curriculum framework for specific content and process goals. Students working in service programs experience not only the commitment to real and meaningful work, but also the joy that comes from helping others. Students sense the authenticity of their work and gain a sense of pride and accomplishment in doing something that really needs to be done.

Taking responsibility for civic duties fosters leadership skills in students. They develop tolerance, respect, and empathic understanding. They also learn to work with others and view situations from many perspectives. In addition, students develop communication skills while interviewing and dialoguing with others. In the best of situations, students become immersed in a labor of love that evokes energy, enthusiasm, and passion.

What Does Service Learning Look and Sound Like?

Service learning manifests itself in community development and beautification projects such as cleaning up neighborhoods, tutoring in literacy programs, reading to the blind, escorting senior citizens to the store, participating in food drives, creating care kits for the homeless, leading graffiti clean-ups, and taking voters to the polls. Creating fliers, press releases, proposals, and fund-raising activities for specific community-related purposes are also service projects related to civic causes.

Service learning encompasses huge areas of concern, including the environment, literacy, government, safety, senior citizens, the hungry and homeless, crime-fighting, and health-related issues. Students develop skills by learning how to file a petition, make a proposal, create a resolution, conduct a survey, lobby for a worthy cause, support or oppose a law, initiate a law, and fundraise.

**Service
Learning**

How Does Service Learning Work?

Service learning, as with other authentic curricular models, adheres to no one formula for successful student endeavors. However, there are elements in the process that occur in most service learning experiences. The actual sequence of events may vary from situation to situation. The critical elements of the service learning experience include the following:

1. Selecting the need for service
2. Finding a community partner
3. Aligning the service experience with educational goals
4. Managing the project or program
5. Fostering reflective student learning throughout the process

Just as with project learning experiences, the multiple intelligences are woven throughout the various stages of the service project. Refer to page 82 in the previous chapter for appropriate alignment of the intelligences as depicted in the Three Story Intellect. Occasionally, particular intelligences are necessary in certain parts of service projects; but, in general, they are infused throughout.

✳ Selecting the Need for Service

The first steps in service learning are (1) knowing what needs to be done in the community and (2) offering students' services. To find out what needs to be done in the community, students can investigate what is already happening. They can survey families, scan local newspapers, catch the evening news on the radio or television, and interview community leaders. There are several service projects that can be discovered from such a search: tutoring younger students; coaching Little League; assisting adults in running after-school programs; working in a library, museum, or park; serving as cadets for rescue squads and hospitals; or organizing fundraisers and community action activities.

Students and teachers should consider the following when deciding on a project: the type of project, the amount of time needed to complete the project, the availability of community support, and the number of service agencies. A rubric might help this decision-making process. The following

**Service
Learning**

illustration demonstrates a simple rubric for logically selecting a service project. Criteria highlighted include interest, need, access, appropriateness, and time frame.

Service Learning Project Selection		
Possible Project or Program_____		
Criteria	1	2	3
INTEREST	High	Medium	Low
NEED	Great	Some	Little
ACCESS	Easy	Works	Difficult
APPROPRIATENESS	Good	Fair	Poor
TIME FRAME	5 Weeks	10 Weeks	Semester

✳ Finding a Community Partner

Visit various agencies and ask them if they would be a partner with the school or class. Remember to take advantage of pro-education community leaders and call on their services.

Students can help contact the agencies, set up appointments, make phone calls, write letters, organize events, set schedules, plan agendas, solve problems, interview agencies, and research leaders to determine their usefulness. Let students take as much responsibility for the project as possible. The more they do, the more they learn.

✳ Aligning Service and Educational Goals

Service goals focus on concepts such as civic responsibility, diversity, economic realities, historical underpinnings, and personal significance. They also focus on life skills such as caring for others, communicating, working in teams, and leading others.

Educational goals have the same focus as service goals, but they also include content-specific goals. For example, a project in which students read to senior citizens includes the educational goals of exposure to various genres of literature (biography, historical fiction, and poetry), understanding of history (historical fiction), and knowledge of science (science-fiction novels). Students might also learn about hearing problems; the aging process; Alzheimer's disease; Parkinson's disease; or working with the blind, disabled, and infirm.

Teachers and students must be clear on the expected outcomes and give deliberate attention to the goals. This is where the specific, targeted academic learning and the transfer of that learning occur.

✳ Managing the Project

Managing a project involves preparing students and a site for the service project, implementing the service, monitoring student learning and desired outcomes, and evaluating the experience for targeted goals. Coordinating these components requires organization, orchestration, persistence, determination, and dedication.

Service Learning

Planning and preparing for the project involves selecting the service project; making site contacts; arranging people, places, and times; getting students to the site; making sure the students know what they're supposed to do; and acting as a liaison between the students and the community partner. Teachers may choose to work in teams or to solicit help from parent volunteers or the service agency.

Monitoring the project includes observing, counseling, giving feedback, dictating site visits, and understanding the goals of the project. The effort it takes to engage students in service learning experiences cannot be underestimated. If not well prepared, teachers can lose their enthusiasm for service projects. It is important to be as prepared as possible and to have a cadre of adult help.

Naturally, the students' work on the project must be assessed and evaluated. Although the assessment and evaluation of the students' work should be planned in the beginning, they are ongoing throughout the project. Students should be held accountable for the amount and intensity of participation, ability to respond to traditional knowledge-based questions, and portfolios of artifacts with reflective notes. Tools that guide the evaluation might include logs and journals, essays, charts of data, surveys and questions, and quizzes and tests that pertain to various educational and service goals.

✳ Fostering Reflective Learning

Student reflection is essential to service learning. By reflecting on their learning throughout the service learning project, students become engaged in deliberate kinds of thoughtfulness that leads to deep understanding and relevant transfer.

When students are immersed in the experience of regularly visiting a senior citizen facility, they come to know personally the concerns of senior citizens. A student who spends time with a senior citizen frustrated about her inability to move about easily, vicariously experiences similar feelings. The student and senior citizen get to know each other and develop a rapport. At this point, the student's learning extends into unforeseen areas.

Students need tools and strategies to document explicit learnings and capture implicit understandings. These tools include learning logs, daily journals, reflective portfolios, time sheets, peer-partner sharing, topical essays, knowledge-based quizzes, comprehensive content-focused tests, projects, class exhibitions, interviews, and conferences.

**Service
Learning**

Throughout the service learning project, students have opportunities to think about, talk about, and openly reflect on their experience. As students make sense of their learning, they internalize new ideas with deep understanding that often does not occur without shepherding. Reflective thought enhances the transfer of learning from a service experience to future situations. When students reflect on their learning, they tend to draw more conclusions, make subtle inferences, sense analogous situations, and stretch learning through insightful generalizations that bring meaning to their learning.

Who Are the Key Players and What Are Their Roles?

Teachers

Teachers and students work together to plan educational strategies that align with the targeted curriculum. The goals, aims, and objectives are then made explicit to the students and the cooperating agencies. Although the teacher is primarily responsible for targeting and incorporating the desired outcomes, the students also need to be informed of the academic goals of the project. Otherwise, the goals may get lost in the excitement of the project.

In addition to being the primary academic advisor, the teacher is a liaison between the school, the students, and the partner agency. Once the academic goals are clear, they are communicated to the agency through the teacher. The students are responsible for knowing these goals well enough to discuss with the agency.

Students

The students' role is to take part in the appropriate tasks and communicate professionally with the agency. The students are active partners in the service project, accountable to the teacher and the service agency. The students are also accountable for academic learning and service to others.

Agencies

The agency's role can vary from director of operations to absentee manager of the project. The agency's role will become clear once the project is arranged. The agency may be quite involved in the project or it may simply administrate through the teacher leader. This varies from project to project, from teacher to teacher, and from agency to agency.

Why Does Service Learning Work?

Learning related to direct involvement in a community service is not a new idea. Rather, it is an authentic model that has been around for the better part of this century. John Dewey's *Democracy and Education* (1916) and

Education and Experience (1963 [1938]) advocate the ideas behind service learning. William Kilpatrick (1918) also promoted the idea of experiential learning and service to society through project learning. Others (Wigginton 1985; Goodlad 1984; Boyer 1984) took Kilpatrick's ideas one step further and advocated social reform through community-oriented projects.

Current literature sheds light on an interesting dichotomy within the service learning experience. J. Kahne and J. Westheimer (1996) discuss in length two goals that often drive the idea of service learning. They divide the motives for service learning into the concepts of *charity* and *change*. According to them, if the driving force is for charitable reasons, the moral element is about giving, the political bent is about civic duty, and the intellectual experience is considered an enhancement to the general curriculum. If, however, the rationale for service learning is derived from the need for social change, the morality is about caring, the politics about social reconstruction, and the intellectual element about transformation.

B. Checkoway (1996) discusses service learning in terms of neighborhood revitalization, community planning, and voter participation projects that are organized around the concept of student workshops. In this context, service learning becomes the catalyst for student involvement in the community in ways that are relevant and civic minded.

In addition, a commentary in *Education Week* (1996) appeared on the debate about students learning by doing in community service projects. Many say people do not learn solely by experience, while others feel that being immersed in the experience creates a deepened understanding of the learning.

Experiential education, as manifested in service learning, project learning, and problem-based learning is also supported by the literature on constructivism (Caine and Caine 1991; Fosnot 1996). Constructivists believe that learning is "constructed" from experiences and making meaning of those experiences. Experiential education works as a curriculum frame because of its authenticity. Regardless of the motivations of charity or change, service learning ignites learning for students in real-life ways.

Service Learning

Service Learning

When Can Service Learning Be Used Effectively?

ELEMENTARY EXAMPLE
Save a Park

Project Summary

Third grade students participate in "Little Litter Day" in which they clean up litter in the park. In addition, students participate in a neighborhood drive to find sponsors in order to fund a "Plant-a-Tree" day. The sponsors are agencies, families, and community groups who support an effort to beautify the park.

✳ Selecting the Need for Service

- ❑ Brainstorm ideas in class.
- ☑ Survey families in the school for ideas.
- ❑ Discuss a teacher-generated idea: *This idea came from a neighbor of the teacher who works for the park district.*
- ❑ Repeat a project from a previous year.
- ❑ Other

Evaluate the idea(s) using a rubric:

Project Title: *Save a Park*	1 (High)	2	3 (Low)	Comments
Interest	X			Third-graders use the park a lot.
Need	X			Park district employee suggested need.
Accessibility	X			Park is next to school.
Appropriateness	X			Third-graders can do clean-up and planting.
Time Frame	X			Time to plan for spring.

✳ Finding a Community Partner

Based on a conversation with a park district employee, the teacher will follow-up with an official call to the park district to request its partnership in this project.

Service Learning

✳ Aligning Service and Educational Goals

Major Subject/Discipline Focus	*Goal(s)*
1. Science	Living things (plants) unit Ecosystem
2. Social Studies	Environment Civic duties Community action
3. Language Arts	Letter writing Persuasive writing News reporting
4. Big Ideas	Think globally, act locally!
5. Life Skills	Cooperation, teamwork, and communication skills

✳ Managing the Service Project

Service Learning

Phase	Planning	Monitoring	Evaluating
1	Contact park district and local nurseries to confirm place.	Review expected procedures with a student for litter clean-ups.	Home groups report back.
2	Introduce project to class. Begin unit on plants.	Get permissions. Send note about clothing etc. to parents.	Revise plan as needed.
3	Divide class into teams for "Little Litter Days." Set up schedule.	Rotate groups through-out litter days program.	Get formal feedback from park district.
4	Arrange for parent helpers. Confirm dates and procedures with park district.	Advertise the sponsor-ship for "Save-a-Park."	Sendd "thank-you's" to parents.
5	Plan sponsorship drive. Work on government unit — rights and responsibilities.	Orchestrate sponsor-ship drive. Collect sponsor information.	Write news articles about project and send out.
6	Plan "Plant-a-Tree Day."	"Plant-a-Tree Day" — Just do it!	Take pictures of group to accompany articles.

IRI/SkyLight Training and Publishing

✳ Fostering Reflective Learning

**Service
Learning**

Learning Lists: Save-a-Park Project	
Vocabulary I learned:	Big ideas to think about:
People I got to know:	Hard Things | Easy Things
Books I read | Video/films I viewed	Questions I still have:

Service Learning

MIDDLE SCHOOL EXAMPLE
Violence: How Can We Kill It?

Project Summary

Middle schools work with local police to establish community awareness fliers that describe ways to deter crime and violence in the neighborhood through community action (e.g., keep lights on; don't leave things visible in car, such as cameras, cell phones, money). In addition to developing informative fliers, students canvas the neighborhood for people willing to display a "neighborhood watch" symbol in their window to indicate the extent of the effort.

✴ Selecting the Need for Service

- ❏ Brainstorm ideas in class.
- ☑ Survey families in the school for ideas: *Family surveys indicated concern about growing number of incidents of "street crimes" in the neighborhood.*
- ❏ Discuss a teacher-generated idea.
- ❏ Repeat a project from a previous year.
- ❏ Other

Evaluate the idea(s) using a rubric:

Project Title: *Violence: How Can We Kill It?*	1 (High)	2	3 (Low)	Comments
Interest	X			Teens are part of this scene.
Need	X			Newspaper articles
Accessibility	X			It's in the neighborhood.
Appropriateness	X			If not us—who? We live here.
Time Frame	X			Fall semester to initiate—but ongoing effort

❋ Finding a Community Partner

Local police are contacted to work with the school. They inform students of "street smart" strategies that deter crime and violence.

❋ Aligning Service and Educational Goals

Service Learning

Major Subject/Discipline Focus	Goal(s)
1. Social Studies	Government services/facilities Responsibilities Court systems, justice Cooperative teamwork
2. Technology	Graphic design Word processing Formatting Type styles
3. Writing	Expository Persuasive
4. Big Ideas	Justice Rights and responsibilities Group action
5. Life Skills	Problem solving Political action Communication skills

**Service
Learning**

✳ **Managing the Service Project**

Phase	Planning	Monitoring	Evaluating
1	Develop and administer survey. Analyze survey results. Decide on project.	Write, edit, refine, and revise survey for parents.	Evaluate survey, results, and final decisions.
2	Initiate project with class through motivating film, song, etc.	Study, read about political action — historically and in news.	Revise plan as needed.
3	Invite police to visit for interviews.	Interview police personnel.	Reflect on information; begin to organize for brochure.
4	Plan brochure, flyer (sketch/draft).	Develop brochure/ flyer on computer.	Evaluate. Revise as necessary.
5	Layout, plan, format.	Distribute flyers. Start with kickoff rally, etc.	Debrief on distribution effort and reactions, etc.

IRI/SkyLight Training and Publishing

✳ **Fostering Reflective Learning**

**Service
Learning**

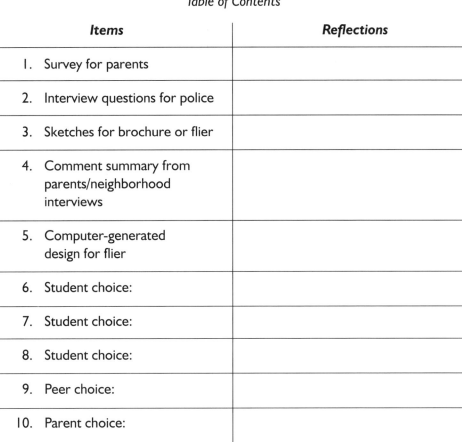

Project Portfolio **Violence: How Can We Kill It?** *Table of Contents*	
Items	***Reflections***
1. Survey for parents	
2. Interview questions for police	
3. Sketches for brochure or flier	
4. Comment summary from parents/neighborhood interviews	
5. Computer-generated design for flier	
6. Student choice:	
7. Student choice:	
8. Student choice:	
9. Peer choice:	
10. Parent choice:	

**Service
Learning**

HIGH SCHOOL EXAMPLE
Old Folks' Tales to Tell

Project Summary

As part of an interdisciplinary project, students in English 10 write biographies of people living in the nursing home, who have interesting stories to tell. Students combine their study of geriatrics in health class and their computer skills for word processing and graphic design. This makes the service learning project a meaningful experience for high-schoolers. The students present their biographies (in book form) at Christmas Tea at the nursing home. The tea is sponsored by the students.

✳ Selecting the Need for Service

- ❏ Brainstorm ideas in class.
- ☑ Survey families in the school for ideas.
- ❏ Discuss a teacher-generated idea.
- ❏ Repeat a project from a previous year: *This is a project repeated every year with this teacher, since the plan is already set with the partner nursing home.*
- ❏ Other

Evaluate the idea(s) using a rubric:

Project Title: *Old Folks' Tales to Tell*	1 (High)	2	3 (Low)	Comments
Interest	X			Students see it as a "tradition".
Need	X			Old folks lonely and isolated.
Accessibility	X			Nearby.
Appropriateness	X			Aging society in America.
Time Frame	X			Fall semester to Christmas.

✳ Finding a Community Partner

The nursing home, adjacent to the school, has participated enthusiastically with the high school English and health teachers for a number of years. The nursing home administrator reports high interest among their clientele, also.

**Service
Learning**

✳ Aligning Service and Educational Goals

Major Subject/Discipline Focus	Goal(s)
1. Health: Geriatrics	Ages Stages of life
2. Social Studies	Demographics Aging Society
3. Literature: Biography	Reading Appreciating
4. Writing	Style Genre
5. Communication Arts (Interview)	Interview questions Face-to-Face communication Interpreting
6. Big Ideas	Loneliness Aging process
7. Life Skills	Relating to others

✳ Managing the Project

Service Learning

Phase	Planning	Monitoring	Evaluating
1	Confirm with nursing home. Introduce project to students.	Prepare students for proper behavior etc. in nursing home.	Review concerns of students.
2	Coordinate health, technology, and English. Begin appropriate units/skills.	Elicit discussion of how to interact with old folks; geriatric knowledge, etc.	Evaluate and reflect on biography as a genre.
3	Set up partnerships with students and old folks. Schedule first interview.	Encourage multiple interviews.	Review notes and generate new questions for old folks.
4	Plan first drafts and other critical due dates.	Monitor student interview progress and student notes, outlines, writing.	Review stages of biography.
5	Set up tea with nursing home. Plan with students.	Solicit help as needed for tea.	Review biographies (final stages now or soon).
6	Plan how to orchestrate "The Day"	Encourage interaction between students and the old folks.	Debrief whole experience.

✳ **Fostering Reflective Learning**

Develop a storyboard that illustrates the construction process for building a biography for the "Old Folks' Tales to Tell" project.

Develop a storyboard of the construction process you experienced as you "built a biography" for the service project "Old Folks' Tales to Tell."

**Service
Learning**

Where Is More Information?

Basic Principles of Curriculum and Instruction by R. W. Tyler

Combining Service and Learning: A Resource Book for Community and Public Service, vol. 1, edited by J. C. Kendall and Associates

"Combining Service and Learning on Campus and in the Community" by B. Checkoway in *Phi Delta Kappan,* May 1996

Constructivism: Theory, Perspectives, and Practice edited by C. T. Fosnot

Dare the Schools Build a New Social Order? by G. Counts

Democracy and Education by J. Dewey

Education and Experience by J. Dewey

How to Establish a High School Service Learning Program by J. Witmer and C. Anderson

"In Service of What? The Politics of Service Learning" by J. Kahne and J. Westheimer in *Phi Delta Kappan,* May 1996

The Kids' Guide to Service Projects by B. Lewis

"Learning Civics in the Community" by S. F. Hamilton and R. Shepherd Zeldin in *Curriculum Inquiry,* vol. 17, 1987

Learning by Giving: K–8 Service Learning Curriculum Guide by R. Cairn

"Learning Leadership" by R. Maher in *Educational Leadership,* December 1985

"A Profile of High School Community Service Programs" by F. M. Newmann and R. A. Rutter in *Educational Leadership,* December 1985

"School-Based Community Service: What We Know from Research Theory" by D. Conrad and D. Hedin in *Phi Delta Kappan,* June 1991

"Service: A Pathway to Knowledge" by D. Hedin and D. Conrad in *Community Educational Journal,* June 1991

"Serving Others Hooks Gifted Students on Learning" by B. Lewis in *Educational Leadership,* February 1996

Sometimes a Shining Moment: Twenty Years at Foxfire by E. Wigginton

Strong Democracy: Participatory Politics for a New Age by B. Barber

"Working at Learning" in *Education Week,* May 1996

Youth Serves the Community by P. Hanna

What's My Thinking Now?

Reflections:

....

....

....

....

....

....

....

Comments:

....

....

....

....

....

....

....

Questions:

....

....

....

....

....

....

....

How Can I Use Service Learning?

Use this outline to apply service learning to your content and classroom.

✳ **Selecting the Need for Service**

....
....
....
....
....
....
....
....
....
....

✳ **Finding Community Partners**

....
....
....
....
....
....
....
....
....
....
....

IRI/SkyLight Training and Publishing

How Can I Use Service Learning?

✳ **Aligning Service with Educational Goals**

....
....
....
....
....
....
....
....
....
....

✳ **Managing the Service Project**

Plan

....
....
....
....

Monitor

....
....
....
....

Evaluate

....
....
....
....

How Can I Use Service Learning?

✳ **Fostering Reflective Learning** (Learning Lists, Storyboards, Portfolios, etc.)

PERFORMANCE LEARNING

I hear and I forget. I see and I remember.
I do and I understand.

—Chinese Proverb

**Performance
Learning**

Performance
Learning

What Is Performance Learning?

Performance learning is as authentic as learning gets. Students actually do
a task or perform certain skills. It also requires them to demonstrate understanding through action. Performance learning is the difference between
talking about fly fishing and actually doing it. The essence of this type of
learning is the performance itself.

Performance learning involves a public appearance of some sort; it is
about genuine achievement. In the case of fly fishing, a mentor or instructor
can witness how skillfully a learner casts her fishing line. The level of learning is obvious to the expert coaching the novice.

Focusing on the execution of a learned skill is a familiar situation in
everyday learning. For example: as a toddler learns to walk and talk, the
performance itself takes center stage. When a person learns how to ride a
horse or swim, performance is the key. Young adults learn to drive cars,
stylists learn how to cut and color hair, computer users learn how to get
online—these are all examples of performance learning that are mea-
sured formally or informally by preset standards, criteria, benchmarks,
or indicators.

What Does Performance Learning
Look and Sound Like?

Competitors in sporting events such as high diving, ice skating, and gymnastics are rated according to the quality of their performances. Actors are
required to audition to demonstrate their acting skills. Orchestral musicians
are seated according to their ability to perform. Following are examples of
performance learning in the school setting.

Examples of Performance Learning in the School Setting

Outdoor education excursions	P.E.
Lab experiments	Dancing
Plays	Home economics
Choir	Keyboarding
Musicals	Computers
Gymnastics	Vocational education
Band	Auto mechanics
Cooking	Photography
Orchestra	Video production
Sewing	Art

Performance Learning

Beyond the schoolhouse door, performance learning permeates the workplace setting and the "common" learning of real life. Office workers learn to use new software programs and their efforts are judged by their performance; architects design buildings and are responsible for their structural soundness and beauty; gas station attendants, store clerks, restaurant servers, and manicurists are all expected to learn by doing. Their work is judged by the quality of their performance.

Performance learning is directly related to skill development. Skill development is associated with mentoring and apprenticing, in which the learner is coached by an expert through a developmental path. As documented by Posner and Keele (1973), a learner passes through a series of stages or phases: novice, apprentice, advanced beginner, competent user, proficient user, and expert. The five stages of development are obviously defined by the level of performance. These stages are similar regardless of the type of skill performed. For example, a figure skater, seamstress, writer, golfer, and gardener all pass through the same stages of development when learning their crafts.

In every area of performance, the stages of development are similar. However, pacing varies greatly from one learner to another. As a student learns, her level of performance and progress is readily tracked by a teacher or mentor. The following outline provides a quick reference for generic performance standards. Specific indicators, of course, should be applied to each category of performance.

Let's follow the development of a golfer, since learning a sport is a performance with which many are familiar. Following are the five stages of a developing golfer.

**Performance
Learning**

Novice

First, the *novice* golfer is introduced to the basics: the proper grip, stance, and swing. Incorporating these three pieces, the learner is expected to practice hitting balls. Many times, however, novices simply practice the grip or the swing and never even try hitting a ball. They may merely try to "groove" the swing or learn to feel the club in a natural grip. In this initial stage, the different pieces are easily isolated for specific practice.

Advanced Beginner

The *advanced beginner* starts to put things together and practice in sequence. At this point, the various pieces begin to flow together. The learner is more concerned about establishing the flow of the performance than getting the desired results. Advanced beginners are concerned about the differences in clubs—the driver, the woods, and the irons—and how to use them appropriately in the game. They are more apt to ask which club to use than to notice how many strokes they take. At this level, the point is to concentrate on understanding how to put the basics together in a beginning game.

Competent User

As learners become *competent,* they begin to care more about the relationship of the skill to the content. They are aware of the context in which the skill is being performed and are interested in understanding what they are doing. Competent golfers often dig into the history of what they are learning about. They experiment with the tools or equipment and read about the experts in the field. They begin to use lingo such as "chipping," "slicing," "hooking." They explore the historical context of "links" and try out the Calloway Big Bertha driver. They read up on books like Harvey Penwick's *Little Red Book of Golf.* Competent golfers are concerned with the big picture and approach the game of golf with an acute awareness of the various elements that impact the overall game. They survey their approach to the next green, notice the hazards, the wind direction, the condition of the ground, and the marked distances. With this information logged, competent users select a club to fit the strategy they have in mind.

Proficient Performer

When learners become *proficient performers,* they move beyond conscious awareness of "how" to do it and glide into an automatic mode. Their movements are connected, relaxed, and synthesized into a smooth and seemingly effortless performance. Proficient performers relate to classes or sets within their performance level. They inherently understand the combinations or sequences that produce a flowing, flawless performance. For example, a proficient performer approaches the tee shot in a similar manner each time, lining up her shot, addressing the ball, practicing her swing, and striking the ball with a subtlety that suggests confidence and skill. The proficient performer often uses a practiced routine or regime that sets the stage for the apparent automaticity of the performance. In a proficient performance, the golfer is accomplished and recognizes that her performance exceeds the norm. She joins the rank of the elite in the field. She may be the club champion or the "lowest handicapper" on the course.

**Performance
Learning**

Expert

Experts often find it difficult to explain what they are doing. In fact, experts often prefer to "show" the sequence. They perform with ease and grace. They often finish with a flourish that expresses the joy of performing at this level of expertise. An expert's performance is so ingrained in the performer that she may actually skip steps in the explanation and jump directly to a solution. For this reason, experts are not always the best teacher. Most learners, however, do want to see an expert perform to scrutinize her performance for its elegant results.

How Does Performance Learning Work?

Performance learning is based on the idea that students learn by doing. Immersion in a complex activity fosters deep understanding and creativity. It is learning not just for a test, but for a lifetime. The onus of responsibility is on the learner and the focus of learning is on transfer into relevant situations.

Grounded in the constructivist philosophy of learning, performance learning comprises the following critical elements: a prompt, a vision, a set of standards, a coaching environment, and a reflection of the learning.

Inherent in the model of performance learning is the framework of Gardner's multiple intelligences. At the heart of performance learning is the inclusion of multiple intelligences. Note the infusion of the intelligences in the various phases of performance learning.

✳ The Prompt

The prompt is the cue for the performance that introduces what the students are expected to do. The classic performance asks students to write a report or give an oral presentation, but performances also include performing a lab experiment, playing a role in a dramatic production, demonstrating a skill in computer class, or simply participating in "show-and-tell" in the primary grades. However, regardless of the type of performance or its complexity, the prompt precedes the action and actually sets the stage for the expected performance.

In the example of a traditional class book report, the prompt is the instructions given to the students. Explaining what is expected provides a big picture of what the learner is to do. In the case of the book report, the teacher

**Performance
Learning**

Critical Elements of Performance Learning

A **PROMPT** of what students are to do

A **VISION** of what adults expect students to do

An **AGREEMENT ABOUT STANDARDS** and levels of quality (rubric)

A **COACHING CONTEXT** to scaffold the learner toward excellence

A **PERFORMANCE** that demonstrates the learning

A **REFLECTION** on results

may prompt the performance by stating the type, timeline, and tenor of the book report. The prompt provides the introductory information necessary for students to begin preparing for the performance.

✳ The Vision

Accompanying the prompt is a vision statement. The vision statement elaborates what the expected performance might look and sound like. It provides an image of the final performance as seen by the adults planning the learning.

In order to help students understand the expectations for their performances, this phase of the prompt may include role-playing, viewing videos of previous student performances, or visiting other classrooms in which students are engaging in similar performances. What is important is that students are exposed to authentic performances that represent the goals of the performance learning.

If students are to give a book report, they can be an audience for another class presenting book reports. Afterward, students may brainstorm ideas about effective ways to give book reports based on how they felt as part of the audience. In some situations, teachers may provide students with lists of ideas to spark their creativity. The students can then rehearse the performance from the performer's viewpoint.

✳ The Standards

Performance Learning

Set standards for the expected performance. They help learners understand what level of performance is "good enough" and what the signs of that level are. If students are to embrace these standards, they must know and understand the indicators of quality. They must be able to tell what makes a performance poor, good, or exceptional. Standards help students and others measure the quality of their performance.

Scoring rubrics help clarify standards. They can be based on a statement of the standard and specify necessary criteria. Indicators can be used to describe the level of achievement for the criteria. Let's use the book report as an example again. The standard for a book report may encompass several criteria, as suggested in the following statement: *The student exhibits knowledge of the reading material through creative oral communication.* This statement addresses criteria concerning understanding, creativity, and oral communication. A scoring rubric delineating these traits might look like this:

	Not Really	*Somewhat*	*A Lot*	*Fully*
Understands the Material				
Demonstrates Unique Methods				
Communicates Effectively				

Using this guide, students self-assess and teachers, peers, or others evaluate the performance based on the predetermined criteria. Naturally, the language in the rubric should be appropriate to the age group and can even be generated by the students themselves. The essence of performance learning is that *the learning is the assessment.*

✳ The Coaching Context

A coaching environment is necessary for a student to give an excellent performance. A coaching environment provides scaffolding that supports the learner. As the student moves through the levels of skill development as delineated by Posner and Keele (1973), his or her learning can be mediated. The coach, expert, or mentor supplies any necessary guidelines and advice for preparing for the performance. This person also provides hints and suggestions for the student as she plans. This kind of coaching is inter-

Performance Learning

woven throughout the performance learning experience and becomes an integral part of the final high-stakes performance that is judged.

The *coaching environment* is referred to in formal settings as an apprenticeship or a practicum. Terms that suggest a coaching context include apprenticeship, journeyman, mentor, and understudy. This coaching context involves a number of explicit and implicit actions or interventions by the teacher. *Explicit* behaviors include discussing with students their intentions; conferencing during various stages of the presentation's development; and checking on timelines, required elements, and students' readiness. *Implicit* coaching behaviors, on the other hand, are manifested in the teacher's visibility, accessibility, and responsiveness to the learner. It is the "managing-by-wandering-around" behavior, identified by Peters and Waterman (1982) in their book *In Search of Excellence.* The teacher intervenes informally and intermittently as needed. The skillful coach is aware of all that is going on with different projects and helps out whenever necessary. The coach asks students about their ideas, looks at their sketches or drawings, provides feedback on critical pieces, and gives advice when needed.

✳ The Presentation

As described earlier, performance learning is rooted in the act or performance itself. Students are immersed in the experience and engaged in the performance. A performance may be as simple as a book report or as complex as a gymnastics routine on a balance beam. Nonetheless, in every instance of performance learning, students are intensely involved in the activity or experience.

Regardless of the performance's level of complexity, students must think critically about the work and approach it with care, creativity, and precision. Performance learning inherently takes learning to another level because the stakes are higher than with traditional pencil-and-paper tasks. The students are accountable for their own learning. They must walk the talk, not just talk the talk. With performance learning, the proof of the students' learning is out in the open for all the world—or at least those in the class—to see.

Just how does this play out with the example of the book report? Imagine that each student performs in individually creative ways. One student creates a puppet of a major character in her report; another incorporates a song into the presentation; and still another student arrives in a period costume, depicting the character and setting of the book. The report may be told in dialect or through a three-dimensional poster. Students may cluster their reports around a common theme or even develop a formal critique of the book on videotape. All of these are examples of authentic performances that relate learning in personally meaningful ways.

✳ The Reflection

If students do not think reflectively about their performance, their experience is incomplete, and it is unlikely that there will be relevant transfer.

Students often make sense of experiences when they reflect on them, because this is when the mind is most likely to make meaningful connections.

There are many appropriate tools for fostering reflection: small group discussions, peer feedback, tailored questions, journals, visual metaphors, dialogues, and essays. Each acts as a cue to the learner for reflective thinking about the performance or presentation. These tools provide a formal platform to encourage thoughtful processing.

Evaluation is built into performance learning because students are expected to show what they know and can do. For students to present a book in an interesting fashion, they must understand the book's essence. Reflecting on the context and meaning of the performance helps the student understand and improve it.

This process for performance learning is a prototype. In reality, the process evolves differently each time it is used. Nonetheless, if the performance learning is well planned by the teacher and well understood by the students, the elements discussed here will usually be present.

**Performance
Learning**

Who Are the Key Players and What Are Their Roles?

The key players for performance learning include the teacher, the student, and the audience. The teacher acts as a mentor, the student as an apprentice and performer, and the audience as judge or critic. A closer look at these roles reveals the complexity of each.

Teachers

Teachers performing as mentors is quite different from teachers performing as instructors. As mentors, teachers are assumed to be proficient performers in the field. Not only are they instructing students in the *rudiments* of the performance, they are also coaching students in the *refinements* of the performance. This mentoring role is easy to spot in a piano teacher, a tennis coach, or a yoga master. A student may eventually surpass her mentor in level and skill, but she still needs an expert to coach her in the intricacies of a skilled performance.

Students

The role of apprentice, unlike the more ordinary role of student learner, involves intense interest and motivation. Students take great risks when preparing for a performance. They are held accountable for their performances, since others will see what they know and can actually do. For example, an actor must know his lines, execute stage directions, use gestures, and articulate the correct tone of voice all at the same time. The performance is a package deal—it must come off as a holistic entity, with all the discrete parts synthesized into a smooth and graceful performance. Therefore, the

**Performance
Learning**

apprentice must stand by to absorb the information and coaching. The intrinsic motivation is a bit more intense with the apprentice role than with the usual learner role.

Audience

The role of the audience is critical to the concept of performance learning. There must be a payoff to the performance. That payoff is usually the appreciation of an audience—its applause, accolades, and critique. Performers want feedback, which the audience provides. Sometimes a judge or a panel provide formal critiques. For instance, a figure skater often has a visible audience who reacts to her performance. Even in the biology laboratory someone provides critical feedback, although that person or persons may not necessarily be a "traditional" audience.

Why Does Performance Learning Work?

The research on performance learning is comprehensive and diverse. It encompasses literature on experiential learning (Dewey [1938] 1963), performance learning (Sizer 1984; Boyer 1984), and/or performance assessment (Wiggins 1993; Stiggins 1991; Hammerman and Musial 1995; Burke 1994), stages of skill development (Polya 1985; Beyer 1987), and the concept of peak performance (Bloom 1981; Csikzentmihalyi 1990).

John Dewey's *Experience and Education* (1963) profiles the ideas gleaned from the progressive schools developed from the University of Chicago Lab School Model. Dewey discusses philosophy of experience and its relation to education. He urges educators to think in terms of how children learn. Of course, he believes that they learn best when they are immersed in authentic learning situations. Sizer (1984) and Boyer (1984) present similar views about a model of learning that is more immersed than Dewey's. In this model, students are actually learning while doing.

In another vein, Grant Wiggins (1993) and Richard Stiggins (1991) speak of the performance as a way to reveal what students really know and what they can do. In fact, they advocate performance as the most authentic form of learning and suggest rigorous scoring devices to measure performances. Along these same lines, Elizabeth Hammerman and Diann Musial (1995) and Kay Burke (1994) delineate examples of performance learning and ways to assess the performances.

Examining performance learning from a more developmental perspective, Polya (1985), Posner and Keele (1973), and Beyer (1987) expose readers to varying schemata involving skill development. The accompanying procedures and heuristics of the researchers shed light on the stages of developing performance skills. In turn, Bloom (1981) and Csikszentmihalyi (1990) expand the concept of performance learning through their writings on peak performance and attaining a "state of flow," or a state of extreme pleasure over the work at hand. Theoretically, the phenomenon of "flow" may provide an additional framework for performance learning that extends the readers' thinking in this area.

Flow

The theory of "flow," according to Csikszentmihalyi (1990), represents a creative immersion in the performance to the extent that the learner or performer reaches a mental state in which everything "flows." When a learner experiences a state of flow, a creative oasis is reached and the performer relishes the complexities and intricacies of the task—free of feelings of frustration, fatigue, or futility.

The model of flow follows a number of simple principles that allow one to transform experiences into this state. They involve goal setting, immersion in the activity, attention to what is happening, and enjoyment of the immediate experience.

Attaining a State of Flow

- Set Goals

- Become Immersed in the Activity

- Pay Attention to What Is Happening

- Enjoy the Immediate Experience

Setting Goals

Goals ranging from lifelong yearnings to short-term, immediate decisions are at the heart of the flow experience. Once the goals are in mind and the challenges are acknowledged, they define a course of action. Yet, it is the self-determined goal that sets the psychological direction for flow to occur. For example, a novice skier must commit to being cold, uncomfortable, awkward, and unsightly. Yet, she knows the goal, skiing down the hill, is worth it.

Becoming Immersed in the Activity

With the goal in hand, the action is in progress. However, one must become immersed in the activity for a state of flow to occur. This immersion is characterized by intense attention, total investment, and full commitment to the task at hand. There must also be a close match between the skillfulness of the participant and the challenge. Otherwise, frustration blocks any possibility of attaining a state of flow. Again, the skier must become completely immersed in the slide, the turn, and the stop in order to gain control of the hill. Then, with the basic skills learned, the skier invites the next challenges. Frustration and fear are removed.

Performance Learning

Paying Attention to What Is Happening

One must be fully aware of what, when, why, and how he or she is doing the task. The depth of awareness is critical, as is understanding and committing to the system within which the task is embedded. Attention to the wholeness of the interaction is key. The skier must be aware of the difficulty of the challenge.

Learning to Enjoy the Immediate Experience

Achieving optimal experience requires determination and discipline. To be able to transform random events into flow, one must reach beyond the normal capacities. Flow drives individuals to great heights of creativity and achievement. It motivates and propels change. But, to create harmony in whatever one chooses to do involves an extreme sense of purpose and self-direction. The skier must push him- or herself to the next level, and, at the same time, relish the slope immediately ahead.

When Can Performance Learning Be Used Effectively?

Performance Learning

ELEMENTARY EXAMPLE
Tumbling

Performance

P.E. demonstration on Parent Night.

✳ **The Prompt**

The teacher introduces second-graders to tumbling by showing them video clips of gymnastic events from the Olympics. The students are expected to perform the tumbling acts, not just know the names of the movements. The teacher sets the stage in the gym by laying out large red mats. Just seeing the mats as they enter the gym gets the students excited about the tumbling unit. The video sequence clinches the prompting phase.

✳ **The Vision**

Developmental stages of expertise among the children is the vision for the performance learning in this second grade tumbling unit. The expectation is that all children will participate and strive to perform as skillfully as possible.

✳ **The Standards**

The standard will be for students to show competency in many movement forms, with developmental proficiency in some movement forms.

Tumbling: *Second grade*	*Oops!*	*Almost*	*Good Job!*	*Yes!*
Approaches	none	stumbles	does it	adds to basic
Executions	can't do	not complete	does it	perfect
Completions (dismounts)	unclear	fumbles	does it	excels
Attitude	frowns	smiles	smiles & waves	smiles, waves, and bows

**Performance
Learning**

✳ **The Coaching Context**

The following guidelines will be used for various tumbling stunts and sequences (forward roll, backward roll, side roll, etc.).

Explanation

Provide a verbal description of the stunt or tumbling act ("Tuck your head, hold your knees, roll forward and over!").

Demonstration

Show the proper form by teacher demonstration or selected student modeling.

Guided Action/Feedback

Direct each second-grader to perform the tumbling sequence with hands-on assistance. Provide specific feedback ("Good speed," "Keep your knees closer together").

Independent Action/Feedback

Allow each student to perform on his or her own. Again, provide specific feedback to encourage improvement in form and functions.

Authentic Performance

Elicit a final "rated" performance from each student on what his or her perceived readiness is for the "real" performance.

The Performance

When possible, create an environment for an authentic performance, such as a Parent Night.

The Reflection

Use Mrs. Potter's Questions to foster student reflection on the performance unit.

Mrs. Potter's Questions

What was I expected to do?

What did I do well?

If I did the same task over, what would I do differently?

What help do I need?

IRI/SkyLight Training and Publishing

MIDDLE SCHOOL EXAMPLE
"How to" Speech

**Performance
Learning**

Performance

Class presentation.

✴ The Prompt

The English teacher gives a "how to" speech entitled "How to Get Rid of the Hiccups." He presents a humorous but effective talk about a number of ways to rid oneself of the annoying predicament of hiccuping.

After the speech, students in the middle school are introduced to the idea that they are to give a "how to" speech. Their first step, of course, is to think about possible topics!

✴ The Vision

The students' speeches are coherent, articulate, and engaging. The performance focuses on teenagers' obsession with appearances, self-consciousness, and peer pressure. By developing the skill and grace for delivering a how-to speech, students experience increased confidence and self-assurance.

✴ The Standards

The standard is to demonstrate coherent thinking and articulate communication skills.

"How to . . ." Speech (Grade 8)	Working on it!	On the right track!	Almost!	Awesome!
Coherent Text	Outline not finished	Outline complete	Outline moved into text format	Speech is prepared.
Articulate Speech	Stock reporter	Weather reporter	Sports announcer	Evangelical!
Engaging to Audience	Eyes glazed over	Attentive	Taking notes	Gotcha! Want to buy your book!

**Performance
Learning**

✸ The Coaching Context

Coach the students through the process of deciding on a topic, researching and developing an outline, writing a coherent speech, and preparing an engaging presentation.

Guiding Questions for Topic

- Do you have five ideas to show me?
- How much do you know about . . . ?
- Is this an idea that interests you? Why?
- Why do you think others might enjoy knowing about . . . ?
- Which is your favorite? Why?
- What's your decision for your topic?

Guiding Timelines

Topic Due:	*October 10*
Research Notes Due:	*October 20*
Outline Due:	*October 25*
First Draft Speech Due:	*November 1*
Final Draft Due:	*November 6*
Rehearsal Date:	*November 13*
Speech Date:	*November 15*

Guidelines for Text

1. Catchy title
2. Interesting introduction
3. Relevant facts
4. Sequential instructions about "how to . . ."
5. Smooth transitions
6. Strong, memorable conclusion

Guidelines for Speaking

1. Strong, original opening
2. Striking visuals
3. Loud voice; eye contact; pacing
4. Humor
5. Audience participation
6. Clinches as closure

✸ The Performance

After the students perform the "how to" speeches, let peers rate the performances based on the predetermined rubric. Use the reflection (see p. 141) for self-assessment.

✳ **The Reflection**

Use de Bono's PMI chart for categorizing the pluses, minuses, and interesting elements of the speeches.

Performance Learning

Plus (+)	
Minus (−)	
Interesting (?)	

**Performance
Learning**

HIGH SCHOOL EXAMPLE
"The Decades in Review"

Performance

Musical production of "The Decades in Review."

✳ The Prompt

Introduce the concept of reviewing previous decades through an audiotape of music from different eras. As the students listen to the montage of musical numbers, they are introduced to the idea of developing a musical production depicting eight historical decades in America.

✳ The Vision

Students will experience history through the music, art, dance, theater, and news commentaries of the day. In essence, the musical will bring history alive in a memorable and meaningful way for high school students.

✳ The Standards

The standard is to demonstrate understanding of historically significant events in America.

"The Decades in Review"	Amateur	Competent	Proficient	Professional
Accuracy of content and context	Confusing	Has a storyline	Engaging effort	Material for network documentary
Musical skills	Playing in Peoria	On the road	Off Broadway	On Broadway
Historic significance	None	Somewhat	Appropriate	Definitely
Teamwork	No team	Team members work independently	Working team	Collaborative, productive team

✳ The Coaching Context

In this type of performance learning, students research, analyze, and synthesize information to sort out the content and context of the musical. They are involved in the hands-on tasks of production, which encompass music, dance, songs, sets, costumes, and props. In addition, they become involved in planning the advertising, programs, and invitations.

For this complex performance, coaching is clustered in three areas and may be facilitated by one or several teachers involved in the performance.

Performance Learning

Guidelines for Historical Content and Context

- Research the decade
- Find newspaper articles, books, and journals of the decade
- Interview people who lived at that time
- Assemble notes
- Create an outline
- Select significant pieces
- Assemble an idea for a production number
- Write a narrative

Guidelines for the Musical Production

- Decide on critical components
- Music
- Dance
- Costumes
- Props
- Setting
- Script
- Cast

Guidelines for Marketing and Promoting Musical

- Design brochure, print, and distribute
- Layout programs, design, print
- Create invitation list
- Do invitations
- Design poster, distribute
- Orchestrate "word-of-mouth" campaign

✳ The Performance

The musical production, which runs for two weekends, is a fund-raiser used to support the next year's production. In this way, the musical is a self-supporting experience that is an authentic performance for students.

**Performance
Learning**

✳ The Reflection

Use a critical review format similar to real reviews. "The Critic's Choice" is completed by each participating student. A brief narrative highlights the strength and weaknesses of the performance.

The Critic's Choice

_____

_____

_____

_____

_____

_____

IRI/SkyLight Training and Publishing

Where Is More Information?

All Our Children Learning: A Primer for Parents, Teachers, and Other Educators by B. Bloom

Assessing Student Performance: Exploring the Purpose and Limits of Testing by G. Wiggins

"Assessment Literacy" by R. Stiggins in *Phi Delta Kappan,* March 1991

Classroom 2061: Activity-Based Assessments in Science Integrated with Mathematics and Language Arts by E. Hammerman and D. Musial

Education and Experience by J. Dewey

Education and Learning to Think by L. Resnick

"Five Standards of Authentic Instruction" by F. M. Newmann and G. G. Wehlage in *Educational Leadership,* April 1993

Flow: The Psychology of Optimal Experience by M. Csikszentmihalyi

Graduation by Exhibition: Assessing Genuine Student Achievement by J. McDonald et al.

High School: A Report on Secondary Education in America by E. Boyer

Horace's Compromise: The Dilemma of the American High School by T. Sizer

Horace's School: Redesigning the American High School by T. Sizer

How to Solve It: A New Aspect of Mathematical Method by G. Polya

In Search of Excellence: Lessons from America's Best Run Companies by T. J. Peters and R. H. Waterman

In Search of Understanding: The Case for the Constructivist Classroom by J. G. Brooks and M. G. Brooks

Inspiring Active Learning: A Handbook for Teachers by M. Harmin

The Mindful School: How to Assess Authentic Learning by K. Burke

Peak performance: Mental Training Techniques of the World's Greatest Athletes by C. A. Garfield

Practical Strategies for Teaching Thinking Skills by B. Beyer

Second Handbook of Research on Teaching edited by Robert M. W. Travers

Student Engagement and Achievement in American Secondary Schools edited by F. M. Newmann

Watershed: A Successful Voyage into Integrative Learning by M. Springer

Performance Learning

What's My Thinking Now?

Reflections:

....
....
....
....
....
....
....

Comments:

....
....
....
....
....
....
....

Questions:

....
....
....
....
....
....
....

IRI/SkyLight Training and Publishing

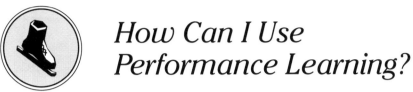

How Can I Use Performance Learning?

Use this outline to apply performance learning to your content and classroom.

✳ **The Prompt**

....
....
....
....
....
....
....
....
....
....
....

✳ **The Vision**

....
....
....
....
....
....
....
....
....
....
....

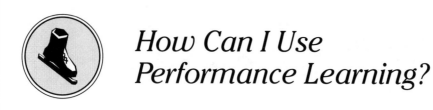

How Can I Use Performance Learning?

✴ **The Standards**

....
....
....
....
....
....
....
....
....
....
....
....
....

✴ **The Coaching Context**

....
....
....
....
....
....
....
....
....
....
....
....
....

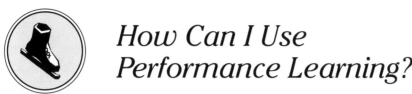

How Can I Use Performance Learning?

✸ **The Reflection**

....
....
....
....
....
....
....
....
....
....

Bibliography

Armstrong, T. 1993. *Seven kinds of smart: Identifying and developing your many intelligences.* New York: Penguin Books

Barber, B. 1984. *Strong democracy: Participatory politics for a new age.* Berkeley: University of California Press.

Barell, J. 1995. *Teaching for thoughtfulness: Classroom strategies to enhance intellectual development.* 2d ed. New York: Longman Publishers.

Barrows, H. 1985. *How to design a problem-based learning curriculum in the preclinical years.* New York: Springer-Verlag.

Beane, J. A. 1993. Problems and possibilities for an integrative curriculum. *Middle School Journal,* September, 18–23.

———. 1995. *Toward a coherent curriculum.* Alexandria, Va.: Association for Supervision and Curriculum Development.

Bellanca, J., and R. Fogarty. 1990. *Blueprints for thinking in the cooperative classroom.* Arlington Heights, Ill.: IRI/SkyLight Training and Publishing.

Berman, S. 1993. *Catch them thinking in science: A handbook of classroom strategies.* Arlington Heights, Ill.: IRI/SkyLight Training and Publishing.

———. 1995. *A multiple intelligences road to a quality classroom.* Arlington Heights, Ill.: IRI/SkyLight Training and Publishing.

Beyer, B. 1987. *Practical strategies for teaching thinking skills.* Needham Heights, Mass.: Allyn and Bacon.

———. 1987. *Practical strategies for teaching thinking.* Boston: Allyn & Bacon.

Bloom, B. 1981. *All our children learning: A primer for parents, teachers, and other educators.* New York: McGraw-Hill.

Bloom, B. S., M. D. Engelhart, E. J. Furst, W. H. Hill, and D. R. Kratwohl. 1956. *Taxonomy of educational objectives: Cognitive domain, handbook I.* New York: David McKay Co.

Boyer, E. 1984. *High school: A report on secondary education in America.* New York: Harper & Row.

———. 1990. Service: Linking school to life. In *Combining service and learning: A resource book for community and public service,* vol. 1, edited by J. C. Kendall and associates. Raleigh, N.C.: National Society for Internship and Experiential Education.

Brooks, J. G., and M. G. Brooks. 1993. *In search of understanding: The case for the constructivist classroom.* Alexandria, Va.: Association for Supervision and Curriculum Development.

Bruner, J. 1973. Readiness for learning. In *Beyond the information given,* edited by J. Anglin. New York: Norton.

Buchler, J. 1954, October. What is a Discussion? *Journal of General Education.*

Burke, K. 1994. *The mindful school: How to assess authentic learning.* Arlington Heights, Ill.: IRI/SkyLight Training and Publishing.

———. 1995. *Managing the interactive classroom: A collection of articles.* Arlington Heights, Ill.: IRI/SkyLight Training and Publishing.

Caine, G. and R. N. Caine. 1991. *Making connections: Teaching and the human brain.* Alexandria, Va.: Association for Supervision and Curriculum Development.

Cairn, R. 1993. *Learning by giving: K–8 service learning curriculum guide.* St. Paul, Minn.: National Youth Leadership Council.

Campbell, B. 1994. *The multiple intelligences handbook.* Stanwood, Wash.: Campbell and Associates, Inc.

Campbell, L. 1992. *Teaching and learning through multiple intelligences.* Seattle: New Horizons for Learning.

Carpenter, T. P., and E. Fennema. 1992. Cognitively guided instruction: Building on the knowledge of students and teachers. In *Curriculum reform: The case of mathematics in the United States,* edited by W. Secada. Elmsford, N. Y.: Pergamon.

Chapman, C. 1993. *If the shoe fits . . . : How to develop multiple intelligences in the classroom.* Arlington Heights, Ill.: IRI/SkyLight Training and Publishing.

Chapman, C., and L. Freeman. 1996. *Multiple intelligences centers and projects.* Arlington Heights, Ill.: IRI/SkyLight Training and Publishing.

Chapman, C., J. Bellanca, and E. Swartz. 1994. *Multiple assessments for multiple intelligences.* Arlington Heights, Ill.: IRI/SkyLight Training and Publishing.

Checkoway, B. 1996. Combining service and learning on campus and in the community. *Phi Delta Kappan,* May, 600–606.

Cohen, M., and E. Nagel. 1934. *An introduction to logic and scientific method.* New York: Harcourt, Brace and World.

Conrad, D., and D. Hedin. 1991, June. School-based community service: What we know from research theory. *Phi Delta Kappan,* 72(10): 44.

Costa, A. L. 1991. *The school as a home for the mind.* Arlington Heights, Ill.: IRI/SkyLight Training and Publishing.

Costa, A. L., ed. 1985. *Developing minds: A resource book for teaching thinking.* Alexandria, Va.: Association for Supervision and Curriculum Development.

Costa, A. L., and R. J. Garmston. 1994. *Cognitive coaching: A foundation for renaissance schools.*

Costa, A. L., J. Bellanca, and R. Fogarty, eds. 1992a. *If minds matter: A foreword to the future (Vol. 1).* Arlington Heights, Ill.: IRI/SkyLight Training and Publishing.

———. 1992b. *If minds matter: A foreword to the future (Vol. 2).* Arlington Heights, Ill.: IRI/SkyLight Training and Publishing.

Counts, G. 1932. *Dare the schools build a new social order?* New York: John Day.

Csikszentmihalyi, M. 1990. *Flow: The psychology of optimal experience.* New York: Harper & Row.

de Bono, E. 1976. *Teaching thinking.* New York: Penguin.

———. 1985. *Six thinking hats.* Boston: Little, Brown.

———. 1992. *Serious creativity: Using the power of lateral thinking to create new ideas.* New York: HarperCollins.

Dewey, J. 1916. *Democracy and Education*. New York: Free Press.

———. 1934. *Art as experience*. New York: Minton, Balch.

———. 1938. *Logic: The theory of inquiry*. New York: Holt.

———. 1963 [1938]. *Education and experience*. New York: Collier Books.

Doll, W. E. 1993. Curriculum possibilities in a 'post' future. *Journal of Curriculum and Supervision*. 277–92.

Doyle, J. 1972. *Educational judgements*. London: Routledge and Kegan Paul.

Education Week. 1996. Working at learning. May 1, 33–36.

Eisner, E. 1985. *Educational imagination: On the design of an evaluation of school programs*. 2d ed. New York: Macmillan Publishing Company.

———. 1994. *Cognition and curriculum reconsidered*. New York: Teachers College Press.

Ennis, R. H. 1969. *Logic in teaching*. Englewood Cliffs, N.J.: Prentice-Hall.

Feldman, D. H. 1986. *Nature's gambit: Child prodigies and the development of human potential*. New York: Basic Books.

Feuerstein, R. 1980. *Instrumental Enrichment*. Baltimore: University Park Press.

Feuerstein, R., Y. Rand., M. Hoffman, and R. Miller. 1980. *Instrumental Enrichment: An intervention program for cognitive modifiability*. Baltimore: University Park Press.

Fogarty, R. 1991. *The mindful school: How to integrate the curricula*. Arlington Heights, Ill.: IRI/SkyLight Training and Publishing.

———. 1994. *The mindful school: How to teach for metacognitive reflection*. Arlington Heights, Ill.: IRI/SkyLight Training and Publishing.

———. 1995. *Best practices for the learner-centered classroom*. Arlington Heights, Ill.: IRI/SkyLight Training and Publishing.

Fogarty, R., and J. Bellanca. 1986. *Catch them thinking: A handbook of classroom strategies*. Arlington Heights, Ill.: IRI/SkyLight Training and Publishing.

———. 1989. *Patterns for thinking: Patterns for transfer*. Arlington Heights, Ill.: IRI/SkyLight Training and Publishing.

———. 1991. *Patterns for thinking: Patterns for transfer*. 2d ed. Arlington Heights, Ill.: IRI/SkyLight Training and Publishing.

———. 1995. *Multiple intelligences: A collection*. Arlington Heights, Ill.: IRI/SkyLight Training and Publishing.

Fogarty, R., and J. Stoehr. 1995. *Integrating curricula with multiple intelligences: Teams, themes, and threads*. Arlington Heights, Ill.: IRI/SkyLight Training and Publishing.

Fogarty, R., D. Perkins, and J. Barell. 1992. *The mindful school: How to teach for transfer*. Arlington Heights, Ill.: IRI/SkyLight Training and Publishing.

Fogarty, R., ed. 1993. *Integrating the curricula: A collection*. Arlington Heights, Ill.: IRI/SkyLight Training and Publishing.

Fosnot, C. T., ed. 1996. *Constructivism: Theory, perspectives, and practice*. New York: Teachers College Press.

Gallagher, S., W. Stepien, and H. Rosenthal. 1992. The effects of problem-based learning on problem-solving. *Gifted Child Quarterly* 36 (4): 195–200.

Gardner, H. 1982. *Art, mind, and brain*. New York: Basic Books.

———. 1983. *Frames of mind: The theory of multiple intelligences*. New York: Basic Books.

———. 1989. *To open minds*. New York: Basic Books.

———. 1993. *Multiple intelligences: The theory in practice*. New York: HarperCollins.

Garfield, C. A., and H. Z. Bennet. 1984. *Peak performance: Mental training techniques of the world's greatest athletes*. Los Angeles: J. P. Tarcher.

Bibliography

Goodlad, J. I. 1984. *A place called school: Prospects for the future.* New York: McGraw Hill.

Hallinger, P., K. Leithwood, and J. Murphy. 1993. *Cognitive perspective on educational leadership.* New York: Teachers College Press.

Hamilton, S. F., and R. S. Zeldin. 1987. Learning civics in the community. *Curriculum Inquiry* vol. 17, p. 407–20.

Hammerman, E., and D. Musial. 1995. *Classroom 2061: Activity-based assessments in science integrated with mathematics and language arts.* Arlington Heights, Ill.: IRI/SkyLight Training and Publishing.

Hanna, P. 1936. *Youth serves the community.* New York: Appleton Century.

Harmin, M. 1994. *Inspiring active learning: A handbook for teachers.* Alexandria, Va.: Association for Supervision and Curriculum Development.

Hedin, D., and D. Conrad. 1987. Service: A pathway to knowledge. *Community Educational Journal.* vol. 15, p. 10–14.

Hoffman, J. 1996, April 18. Letter to author regarding "Shoebox Science." Janesville, Wisconsin, Franklin Middle School.

Holtkamp, S. 1995, June. Santa Margaurita High School's Integrated Curriculum Department Fair.

Isaac, S., and W. Michael. 1981. *Handbook in research and evaluation: For education and the behavioral sciences.* San Diego: Edits.

Jacobs, H. H., ed. 1990. *Interdisciplinary curriculum: Design and implementation.* Alexandria, Va.: Association for Supervision and Curriculum Development.

Johnson, D., and R. Johnson. 1987. *Learning together and alone: Cooperative, competitive, and individualistic learning.* Englewood Cliffs, N.J.: Prentice Hall.

Johnson, R., and D. Johnson. 1986. *Circles of learning: Cooperation in the classroom.* Alexandria, Va.: Association for Supervision and Curriculum Development.

Jones, B. F., A. Palincsar, D. S. Ogle, and E. G. Carr. 1987. *Strategic teaching and learning: Cognitive instruction in the content areas.* Alexandria, Va.: Association for Supervision and Curriculum Development.

Jones, B. F., M. R. Amiran, and M. Katims. 1985. Teaching cognitive strategies and text structures. In *Thinking and learning skills: Relating instruction to research,* vol. 1., edited by J. Segal, S. F. Chapman, and R. Glaser. Hillsdale, N.J.: Lawrence Erlbaum.

Joyce, B., and M. Weil. 1980. *Models of teaching.* 2d ed. Englewood Cliffs, N.J.: Prentice-Hall, Inc.

Kagan, S. 1992. *Cooperative learning.* San Juan Capistrano, Calif.: Resources for Teachers, Inc.

Kahne, J., and J. Westheimer. 1996. In service of what? The politics of service learning. *Phi Delta Kappan,* May, 593–99.

Kendall, J. 1990. Introduction. In *Combining service and learning: A resource book for community and public service,* vol. 1, edited by J. C. Kendall and associates. Raleigh, N.C.: National Society for Internships and Experiential Education.

Kilpatrick, W. 1918. The project method. *Teachers College Record,* September, 319–35.

Kotulak, R. 1996. *Inside the brain: Revolutionary discoveries of how the mind works.* Kansas City, Mo.: Andrews and McMeel.

Kovalik, S. 1993. *ITI: The model: Integrated thematic instruction.* Oak Creek, Ariz.: Books for Educators.

Lewis, B. 1995. *The kids' guide to service projects.* Minneapolis: Free Spirit Publishing.

———. 1996. Serving others hooks gifted student on learning. *Educational Leadership*, February, 70–74.

Lipman, M. 1967. *What happens in art.* New York: Applerton-Century-Crofts.

———. 1973. *Contmeporary aesthetics.* Boston: Allyn and Bacon.

———. 1974. *Harry Stottlemeier's discovery.* Upper Montclair, N.J.: Institute for the Advancement of Philosophy for Children.

———. 1976. *Lisa.* Upper Montclair, N.J.: Institute for the Advancement of Philosophy for Children.

———. 1978. *Suki.* Upper Montclair, N.J.: Institute for the Advancement of Philosophy for Children.

———. 1979. *Mark.* Upper Montclair, N.J.: Institute for the Advancement of Philosophy for Children.

Lipman, M., A. M. Sharp, and F. S. Oscanyan. 1977. *Ethcal inquiry: Instructional manual to accompany Lisa.* Upper Montclair, N.J.: Institute for the Advancement of Philosophy for Children.

———. 1980. *Philosophy in the classroom.* Philadelphia: Temple University Press.

Loundsbury, J. H., ed. 1992. *Connecting curriculum through interdisciplinary instruction.* Columbus, Ohio: National Middle School Association.

Maher, R. 1985. Learning leadership. *Educational Leadership,* December, 59–62.

Martin, H. 1995. *Multiple intelligences in the mathematics classroom.* Arlington Heights, Ill.: IRI/SkyLight Training and Publishing.

———. 1996. *Integrating mathematics across the curriculum.* Arlington Heights, Ill.: IRI/SkyLight Training and Publishing.

Marzano, R. et al. 1988. *Dimensions of thinking.* Alexandria, Va.: Association for Supervision and Curriculum Development.

McDonald, J., and others. 1993. *Graduation by exhibition: Assessing genuine student achievement.* Alexandria, Va.: Association for Supervision and Curriculum Development.

Merenbloom, E. Y. 1991. *The team process: A handbook for teachers.* Columbus, Ohio: National Middle School Association.

Miles, M., and A. M. Huberman. 1984. *Qualitative data analysis: A sourcebook of new methods.* Beverly Hills: Sage Publications.

Murphy, J. 1991. *Restructuring schools: Capturing and assessing phenomena.* Nashville, Tenn.: National Center of Educational Leadership, Vanderbilt University.

Newmann, F. M. 1991. Linking restructuring to authentic student achievement. *Phi Delta Kappan* 72 (6):458–63.

Newmann, F. M., and G. G. Wehlage. 1993. Five standards of authentic instruction. *Educational Leadership,* April, 8–12.

Newmann, F. M., G. G. Wehlage, and S. D. Lamborn. 1992. The significance and sources of student engagement. In *Student engagement and achievement in American secondary schools,* edited by F. M. Newmann. New York: Teachers College Press.

Newmann, F. M., and R. A. Rutter. 1985. A profile of high school community service programs. *Educational Leadership,* December, 65–71.

Nickerson, R., D. Perkins, and E. Smith. 1985. *The teaching of thinking.* Hillsdale, N.J.: Lawrence Erlbaum Associates.

Ogle, D. 1986. K-W-L: A teaching model that develops active reading of expository text. *The Reading Teacher* 37(6): 564–70.

Parnes, S., R. Noller, and A. Biondi. 1977. *Guide to creative action.* New York: Scribner's.

Paul, R. 1987. Dialogical thinking: Critical thought essential to the acquisition of rational knowledge and passions. In *Teaching thinking skills: Theory and practice,* edited by J. Baron and R. Sternberg. New York: W. H. Freeman.

Perkins, D. N. 1988. *Thinking frames.* Paper presented at ASCD Conference on Approaches to Teaching Thinking, Alexandria, Va.

———. 1992. *Smart schools: From training memories to educating minds.* New York: Free Press.

Peters, T. J., and R. H. Waterman. 1982. *In search of excellence: Lessons from America's best run companies.* New York: Warner Books.

Piaget, J. 1952. *The origins of intelligence in children.* New York: International Universities Press.

———. 1958. *The birth of logical thinking from childhood to adolescence.* New York: Basic Books.

Polya, G. 1988. *How to solve it: A new aspect of mathematical method.* 2d ed. Princeton, N.J.: Princeton University Press.

Posner, M. I., and S. W. Keele. 1973. Skill learning. In *Second handbook of research on teaching,* edited by Robert M. W. Travers. Chicago: Rand McNally College Publishing Co.

Postman, N., and C. Weingartner. 1969. *Teaching as a subversive activity.* New York: Delacorte.

Raths, L. E., et al. 1967. *Teaching for thinking.* Columbus: Merrill.

Renzulli, J. S. 1994. *Schools for talent development: A practical plan for total school improvement.* Mansfield Center, Conn.: Creative Learning Press.

Renzulli, J. S., and L. H. Smith. 1979. *A guidebook for developing individualized educational programs (IEP) for gifted and talented students.* Mansfield Center, Conn.: Creative Learning Press.

Resnick, L. 1987. *Education and learning to think.* Washington, D.C.: National Research Council.

Schrenko, L. 1994. *Structuring a learner-centered school.* Arlington Heights, Ill.: IRI/SkyLight Training and Publishing.

Sizer, T. 1984. *Horace's compromise: The dilemma of the American high school.* Boston: Houghton Mifflin.

———. 1992. *Horace's school: Redesigning the American high school.* Boston: Houghton Mifflin.

Springer, M. 1994. *Watershed: A successful voyage into integrative learning.* Columbus: National Middle School Association.

Stanciak, L. A. 1996. *The newsletter of the interdisciplinary curriculum and instruction network.* Palos Heights, Ill.: Interdisciplinary Curriculum and Instruction Network.

Stepien, W., and S. Gallagher. 1993. Problem-based learning: As authentic as it gets. *Educational Leadership,* April, 25–28.

Stepien, W., S. Gallagher, and D. Workman. 1993. Problem-based learning for the traditional and the interdisciplinary classrooms. *Journal for Gifted Education* 16(4): 338–57

Sternberg, R. J. 1985. *Beyond I.Q.: A triarchic theory of human intelligences.* New York: Cambridge University.

———. 1990. *Metaphors of mind: Conceptions of the nature of intelligence.* New York: Viking Penguin.

Stiggins, R. 1991. Assessment literacy. *Phi Delta Kappan,* March, 534–39.

Sylwester, R. 1996. *Explosion of neurons.* Alexandria, Va.: Association for Supervision and Curriculum Development.

Torrence, E. P. 1963. *Education and the creative potential.* Minneapolis: University of Minnesota Press.

Tyler, R. W. 1949. *Basic principles of curriculum and instruction.* Chicago: The University of Chicago Press.

Vygotsky, L. S. 1978. *Mind in society: The development of higher psychological processes,* edited by M. Cole, V. John-Steiner, S. Scribner, and E. Souherman. Cambridge, Mass.: Harvard University Press.

Wasserman, S. 1991. *Cases for teaching in the secondary school.* Coquitlam, B.C.: CaseWorks.

———. 1994. Using cases to study teaching. *Phi Delta Kappan,* April, 602–04.

Wiggins, G. 1993. *Assessing student performance: Exploring the purpose and limits of testing.* San Francisco: Jossey-Bass.

Wigginton, E. 1985. *Sometimes a shining moment: Twenty years at Foxfire.* Garden City, N.Y.: Anchor Press/Doubleday.

Williams, R. B. 1993. *More than 50 ways to build team consensus.* Arlington Heights, Ill.: IRI/SkyLight Training and Publishing.

Witmer, J., and C. Anderson. 1994. *How to establish a high school service learning program.* Alexandria, Va.: Association for Supervision and Curriculum Development.

Index

There are
one-story intellects,
two-story intellects, and
three-story intellects with skylights.

All fact collectors, who have no aim beyond their facts, are

one-story minds.

Two-story minds
compare, reason, generalize,
using the labors of the fact collectors
as well as their own.

Three-story minds
idealize, imagine, predict—their best illumination
comes from above,

through the **skylight**.

—Oliver Wendell Holmes

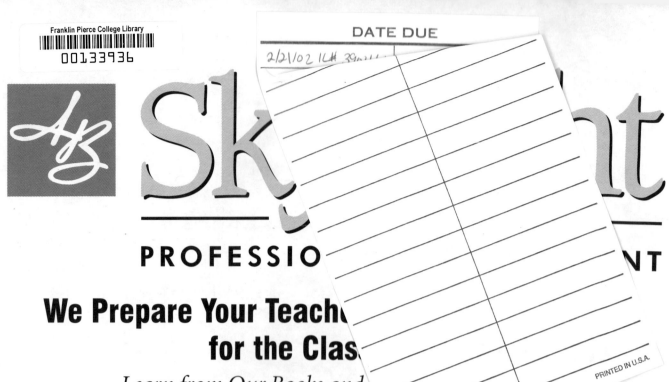

Sk... ...t

PROFESSIO ... NT

We Prepare Your Teach... for the Clas...

Learn from Our Books and ...

Ignite Learning in Your School or District.

SkyLight's team of classroom-experienced consultants can help you foster systemic change for increased student achievement.

Professional development is a process not an event. SkyLight's experienced practitioners drive the creation of our on-site professional development programs, graduate courses, research-based publications, interactive video courses, teacher-friendly training materials, and online resources—call SkyLight Professional Development today.

SkyLight specializes in three professional development areas.

Specialty #  **Best Practices**

...**model** the best practices that result in improved student performance and guided applications.

Specialty #  **Making the Innovations Last**

We help set up **support** systems that make innovations part of everyday practice in the long-term systemic improvement of your school or district.

Specialty #  **How to Assess the Results**

We prepare your school leaders to encourage and **assess** teacher growth, **measure** student achievement, and **evaluate** program success.

Contact the SkyLight team and begin a process toward long-term results.

SkyLight
Professional
Development

2626 S. Clearbrook Dr., Arlington Heights, IL 60005
800-348-4474 • 847-290-6600 • FAX 847-290-6609
info@skylightedu.com • www.skylightedu.com